ACTION STATIONS

A field manual
on stress for high
performers and leaders

By Nigel Cushion

100 ways to deal with stress
and improve performance.

Action Stations
A field manual on stress for high performers and leaders.

Published by Nelsonspirit Publishing, a trading name of Nelsonspirit Limited.

Designed, typeset and printed by Hollinger Print, Norwich, England.
www.hollinger.co.uk

A CIP record for this book is available from the British Library.

ISBN 978-1-9160039-0-3

WHO IS THIS FIELD MANUAL FOR?

This field manual is for anyone who is in a performance role, or is leading, or both. It is also for my sons Ben and Jake, and all the future leaders.

At some point in the modern world, you are likely to come under severe and sustained stress, and what I call, a 'mental health attack'. This manual helps you deal with this attack when it comes. Managing stress and mental health for yourself, and anyone following you, lie at the heart of both high performance and leadership. In the last few years I have mentored many leaders, and one issue has emerged as critical: the effect that stress is having on us all. With the impact of information technology on our working lives, mental health attacks are likely to be more frequent and more severe for leaders, and anyone in a performance role.

Performance roles include being:

The CEO of a large organisation
The owner-manager of a small business
The CEO of a charity
The Managing Director of a family business
An athlete
An actor
An entrepreneur
A youth leader
A student aiming for good grades
A carer
A teenager maturing into adulthood
A volunteer in a community organisation
A parent, balancing work and family
A doctor, nurse, or teacher
A member of the armed forces
A coach, mentor or consultant
A self employed worker
A Head Teacher
A senior manager in a large organisation
A coachman or a king.

This manual helps you better understand 'mental health attack'; provides *100 ACTION STATIONS!* points for you to deploy; and it challenges leaders to be armed and ready for the future. I have been lucky enough to receive inspiration from many heroes and leaders. My aim with this manual is to pass this on, to help you perform better and lead better. It's time for us all to get to ACTION STATIONS!

DEDICATED TO:

My grandfather Private Albert Edward Cushion, 2 Battalion Norfolk Regiment, who 100 years ago returned from the Great War. He was one of the few survivors of the Siege of Kut Al Amara, the desert death march, and 2 years in a concentration camp in Mesopotamia. I reflect when I have a bad day, it can be nowhere near as bad as many days of his. And then I get to ACTION STATIONS!

ENDORSEMENTS

"A fascinating read. Nigel addresses an increasingly important subject for today's leaders, combining recognised theory with personal experience and his extensive leadership experience and journey. The 100 actions he outlines are truly practical and brought to life with real-life stories from past and present which are compelling in their own right." **Michael Morecroft, Commercial Operations Director, Janus Henderson, Investment Managers.**

"Nigel Cushion is a business leader with immense wisdom and a huge heart. The insights he shares include real gems that will benefit us all." **Pete Ashby, Leadership Programme Director, St George's House, Windsor Castle**.

"This manual, provides many anecdotes, and practical tips that are proven to make a positive difference to a person's wellbeing. I believe this is a useful resource to help maintain balance through life's challenges." **Tim Newenham, Olympic Coach.**

"It is not often Alex Ferguson, Ernest Shackleton, King Arthur, Mahatma Gandi and Edith Cavell end up in the same place, but this manual draws on their experiences and the lessons they learned to helpfully equip 21st Century man and woman to navigate the pressures of today." **Peter Hinton, Associate Fellow, Saïd Business School, University of Oxford.**

"Nigel takes the key issue of the day and provides honest, authentic and helpful practical actions borne out of personal experience and calls on the heroes of history to guide and support modern leaders. An essential read for anyone under fire." **Stuart Rimmer, CEO, Coach, and Educationalist.**

"This manual is the next best thing to having your own role models, who can guide and support you through managing stress effectively. Powerful, perceptive and practical." **Sue Stockdale, Polar Explorer, Speaker and Leadership Coach.**

"Having had a large amount of experience in dealing with stressful situations throughout his life, Nigel is able to share these experiences combined with current research and wider literature, to provide a huge range of pro-active strategies within a well-researched and easily understandable framework; allowing the reader the opportunity to ACTION the best fits for them. Personally, Nigel has always been a great source of strength for myself and my family. I hope that by Nigel sharing what he has learnt through this manual, that others will be as lucky as I to gain strength from his support to help fight against one of the biggest medical epidemics we have faced in recent times." **Joe Cowan, Director of Sport, Norwich School.**

"Informative, innovative and pragmatic. Every serious professional should have this manual within easy reach on their bookshelf." **Lt. Col. Matt Woodeson, British Army.**

"It is my great privilege to know Nigel as a teacher, mentor and friend. His warmth, enthusiasm and curiosity are infectious; he is a man who navigates life with a moral compass that never wavers from true north. It was with much excitement that I learned that he had decided to commit some of his thoughts and experiences to paper. This manual does not disappoint; it is brimming over with everyday wisdom and practical suggestions for how we might all better navigate our lives when things seem bleak. If you ever get a chance to meet Nigel in person, or to hear him talk, grab the opportunity with both hands. Until then, the manual you have in your hands, is a wonderful introduction to his message and vision." **Andy Fisher, Teacher, and Founder of The Hero Forge.**

"A great read with fantastic insights beneficial to all, from leaders in industry to those at the start of their careers. Nigel Cushion draws on both personal experience and those of key figures to equip his readers with the ability to deal with the stress that comes with striving to lead and perform." **Nihar Navapurkar, Management Consultant, KPMG.**

"Nigel Cushion has succeeded in writing a manual about a serious issue in an amusing and entertaining way. It is practical, and holistic, for it draws not only on the author's personal experience but on stories from just about every walk of life. If 100 actions seem like a lot, don't worry – there is a clear structure and the manual invites browsing. I wondered at every point what kind of example would be coming next. It has something for everyone." **Stephen Bungay, Author and Historian.**

"Nigel deserves our gratitude for sharing his experiences so we all might benefit. This manual, with its action oriented advice, comes at the perfect time to guide those who are searching for answers as to how we can thrive in this high-pressure world." **Tim Sweeting, Chief Executive. YMCA Norfolk.**

"To operate at the top of their game, leaders need to focus on their wellbeing – especially their mental health. This manual provides concrete, practical steps that we can all take as leaders to safeguard and enhance our mental wellbeing." **Dave King, Vice President, International Oil & Gas Company.**

"*Nigel in a nutshell* ... this manual made me smile. It sums up the skills, knowledge, passion and characteristics of Nigel and his love of developing and supporting leaders. Nigel was the catalyst for the development of my personal leadership journey and belief in myself. His contagious positive mental attitude combined with his spritely personality lifted me and took me forward, and I am sure he will enhance the lives of many other leaders with this charming, user-friendly, can-do-it action manual!" **Lisa Vescio, Founder and Managing Director, Milestones Mental Health Hospital.**

"A manual with practical information and actions for today's leaders to tackle an important and serious issue. The actions outlined are practical and often relate to Nigel's personal experience, making it compelling and easy reading. A really helpful manual which can be referred to again and again." **Daniel Fordham, Operation Director, NPS Property Consultants.**

"This deeply personal insight into a great business mind, provides applied techniques to both counter the stressors of the modern world, and improve your performance as a leader. No matter what your background, this manual will benefit you and those around you. Full of interesting stories and amusing anecdotes, it is also simply a bloody good read!" **Major Rob Smit, Former Infantry Officer on Operations; Apache Attack Helicopter Pilot; British Army.**

"A passionate and reasoned analysis of one of the most overlooked and underrated threats to quality of life in the modern age. Nigel manages to strike the fine balance between explanation and inspiration as he shines a light on key techniques that can help us all to combat excessive stress in our daily lives." **Mark Carter, a senior partner in an international consultancy.**

"Mental Health conditions are thankfully now more widely acknowledged as common place, yet the effects and impact on people's lives are very different. This manual gives a range of tools that can be used to make life easier, whilst they won't ALL work for everyone, if just a couple help then this manual is a great resource." **Ben Handford, Managing Director, Naked Marketing.**

"Truly a survival manual for all leaders and potential leaders! We all think our roles are challenging and we all take down those two All Blacks daily! Many of us will spot the third break off from the pack, see the danger but fail to call for reinforcements. This manual helps you recognise those danger signs, encourages you to call for help and provides multiple strategies for when the attack becomes overwhelming. I have found this "manual" personally very enlightening, fostering a positivity to situations that seem insurmountable, supporting a self-care approach but sign-posting the place, time and need for expert help on occasions. Many of my patients will benefit as I have, from reading this." **Dr John Applegate, GP.**

"This is a manual of great value to you. Nigel leads you through thought and assessment and takes you to solutions and practical options. The 100 actions inspire. I have been lucky to work in the natural environment which gives you a multitude of de-stressing options but it takes a manual like this to make sure you follow a pattern, learn and deliver a remedy for you. Nigel's own experience here shared, given his respected leadership, is inspiration for us all to perform better and look after ourselves." **Richard Powell OBE, Director, History of Advertising Trust.**

"Nigel's journey is open and honest, showing that he really understands the challenges and stresses of leadership, in our professions and our private lives, and offers a wide range of solutions that only someone who has lived the experience could do. If you're stressed when you start reading, by the end of the manual you will realise you're not unique, you're not alone and you're not trapped. This is the sustainable exit strategy." **James Kearns, CEO Build Charity**.

THANKS

I would like to thank the people that have helped me in my life lead and perform, and when my own mental health has been under attack, helped me get to ACTION STATIONS!

Particularly:

My mum and dad, and family, who have encouraged me to develop lifelong tools to generate positive mental health; and my wife and best friend Nicki, who inspires me every day to maintain my mental health.

My late friend and mentor American Dr Hal Belknap, Physician, Scoutmaster and Community Leader, a world class role model in helping others achieve great mental health and performance.

My friend and author DJ Taylor, for his encouragement and guidance.

Finally, all the fantastic leaders I have worked with from business, charities and public service who have inspired me and inspire their followers each day, and in doing so, help deliver outstanding performance to their enterprises and our community.

Nicki and Nigel – at Norfolk and Norwich Festival.
Love and 100 actions.

CONTENTS

PART ONE:
UNDERSTANDING STRESS

CHAPTER 1: INTRODUCTION

What do we mean by "stress" and "mental health"? There is a huge catalogue of reference material on what each of these terms means. I am less concerned with what we call something, more concerned with what are going to do about it, so I am going to cover this ground quickly.

STRESS

The Oxford English dictionary defines stress as *"a state of mental or emotional strain or tension resulting from adverse or demanding circumstances".* You might prefer a more medical definition of: *"a physical, chemical or emotional factor, to which an individual fails to make a satisfactory adaptation, and which causes physiological tensions that may be a contributing cause of disease".* You might prefer a definition where the focus is more on the external force such as *"a threat, real or implied, to the psychological or physical integrity of an individual".* Or you might prefer the engineering approach *"where an external force exerts deforming structural strain on an object"* ... from the Latin stringere – meaning to tighten. I like this one, as the opposite to 'tighten' is to 'loosen' or 'relax'.

Whatever definition you prefer, the key thing seems to be the impact that something external to us, has on us.

MENTAL HEALTH

Much of the narrative around mental health is on diagnosis and description, and our common parlance in this area is confusing. The term mental health is usually used in an isolated sense i.e. it is health, separate from physical health or other types of health. When we say health we usually mean physical health. Interestingly the word health actually derives from the old English word, hælth, of Germanic origin, meaning 'of the whole'. Health, according to the dictionary, is the "state of being free from illness or injury". Mental health also usually carries negative connotations, meaning poor health or illness. Most of the narrative around mental health focuses on extremely poor mental health associated with conditions or syndromes, which require a medical response. The World Health Organisation defines good mental health as *"A state of wellbeing in which every individual realises his or her own potential, can cope with the normal stresses of life, can work productively and fruitfully and is able to make a contribution to her or his community."* Alternatively, from Huppert 2008:*"Wellbeing is your ability to feel good, and function effectively."* At a first principles level, FREEDOM is one of the highest human values, and illness is one of the greatest human curses. So, health can be argued to be one of the greatest human states. We all know that when we are free, and when we are not ill, we have the best chance to reach happiness, another basic human value. Our National Health Service (NHS) is built around a General Practice (GP) referral system focusing on physical health, although most GPs I have spoken to say that over a third or more of the patients they see, have a mental health element to their condition. Differences between states and conditions might interest clinicians but as a practitioner I just want to be free from illness, feel better and perform better. I need practical things that work and I'm not too bothered why it does or does not, or what it's called. I will leave that to others to deal with.

Before proceeding further, I would like to introduce three concepts which I think will be helpful:

ACTION STATIONS

Firstly – I am borrowing from the Royal Navy the concept of "ACTION STATIONS". (Aka STAND TO - Army; and BATTLE STATIONS - United States). This is what happens when an enemy is attacking or is about to attack. The action stations concept presents a place, a state of readiness, and a sequence of expected actions in response to an incoming situation. I have found it useful to think of poor mental health as the enemy and therefore you need to recognise that you are under attack (or are about to be), and bring yourself to a higher state of readiness and then engage in steps to respond. Being in battle is substantively different from other states an army finds itself in, such as preparation, leave, training, etc. If the enemy are attacking they will do damage, even if you do not recognise you are under attack, or recognise but fail to respond. We need to raise our game and be ready to repel. Poor mental health is an emergency, which we need to sort out. Failure to do so will have long term consequences. The good news is that by viewing it as a short-term emergency, it can galvanise us into action. We can respond to it and sort it out. It requires recognition, energy, focus and discipline to respond, and practising the techniques that will help you. If you are under severe and sustained stress, what I call Mental Health Attack - get to ACTION STATIONS!

HEROES

Secondly – if we are to effectively deal with mental health attack, we need to challenge the way we THINK about it. Improving your mental health starts by improving your thinking. And then doing STUFF. To help us think differently, and do stuff, I have included examples and inspiration from "heroes". Some of these you will be familiar with from history, and some are not so famous. The reason for including these is to make this manual a more interesting read, and in my day job of mentoring leaders, I have often found it useful to pick a story of a hero or leader of the past as an inspiration to make a particular leadership or management point. Those who work with me will know that history is a love of mine. The choice of heroes is completely personal. All those listed are people that I have taken some inspiration from. They might not all inspire you. And, of course, they are biased. Much of our life-shaping inspiration comes from our childhood, and mine was that of a Norfolk boy growing up in the 1970s.

Some interesting work on heroes has been done by Andy Fisher, an inspirational school teacher, whose mission through "The Hero Forge" is to "provide 'everyday heroes' with the tools, skills and attributes needed to make a difference in the world". He defines a hero as "someone who chooses to act in the service of the greater good, despite personal risk or sacrifice". But most of us fail to be heroes, even though we have the potential to be, as we are paralysed into inaction by the bystander effect. The bystander effect means that: we are busy and distracted and therefore ignorant of what is going on around us. We are disconnected which makes us indifferent to those around us. We are fearful and unprepared, making us incapable to respond. We are obedient conformers, making us insignificant. Andy suggests these can be addressed by being curious, connected, courageous and committed. Andy inspired me to apply the bystander effect and map it into this manual.

The problem: Dimensions of the Bystander effect: (from Andy)	The problem: Implications for stress and mental health:	The Solution: The Bystander effect can be addressed by: (from Andy)	The Solution: Implications for stress and mental health:
Ignorant	We fail to recognise the worsening of our own health.	Be curious (discernment)	Read this manual, and be inspired by others to take action. Practise the Action Stations points under the heading RECOGNITION. Don't be ill through ignorance, be well through wisdom. Help others be well.
Indifferent	We fail to recognise the worsening of the health of others.	Be connected (empathy)	Pass the Action Stations points in this manual under the heading RECOGNITION, to those around you.
Incapable	We don't know what to do to improve our mental health.	Be courageous	Apply the Action Stations points under the headings RECOVERY, and RESPONSE. Take action now.
Insignificant	We rely on the experts to tell us and make us better.	Be committed (governance)	Don't just rely on the experts. Take personal responsibility for deploying the Action Stations points under the heading RECOVERY, and RESPONSE consistently over the long run.

This manual is designed to help you become an 'everyday hero' in relation to your own health. Don't be a bystander, take action to deal with stress and improve your health. Be curious, connected, courageous and committed to be inspired. Then deploy the 100 ACTION STATIONS! points.

Further reading: The Hero Forge. Andy Fisher. 2017.

"Andy Fisher – of The Hero Forge –
addressing the bystander effect"

THREE RS

Thirdly – there is a really important point about deployment that you need to understand. The action you can take to help with your stress and mental health can be split into three phases: Recognition, Recovery and Response.

1. **Recognition** – accepting that you are under a mental health attack and viewing it in different and new ways to help you deal with it.
2. **Recover** – working on actions that give you time and space to think and rest, so that you are able to stop things getting worse and put you in a position to move forward.
3. **Respond** - responses that will directly help you get better.

Most of us make a complete mess of managing the Three Rs, and in doing so we often hold back our health and sometimes make it worse. This is what typically happens (and needs to be avoided):

Recognition ERROR (R1) – we fail to recognise the fact that our health is under attack, or if we do, we underestimate it and / or fail to take it seriously. Most of us do very little to manage our increase in stress, and we do very little for a long and sustained period! We might be subconsciously managing stress well, but more likely we are not, and we delude ourselves that we are fine.

Recovery ERROR (R2) – we do not give ourselves time to recover and "energise up" to deal with the threats. We often miss this recovery phase and try to go straight from late recognition to emergency response!

Response ERROR (R3) - we respond too late with too little force. When things get extreme, we try to take extreme (and often not the right) action. Too little, too late.

In practice, these errors compound each other: Poor stress response = R1 x R2 x R3. The first step on winning the health battle is to reverse all this.

This is what we need to do:

1. **Recognition** – to recognise the fact that your health is under attack. The earlier the better. Accept it. Face it. It's normal. Take it seriously. Preventative health action is always better than corrective action. Accept that you need to get to "Action Stations".
2. **Recovery** – give yourself time to recover and energise up to deal with the threats. Do not move straight into emergency response without ensuring you have the energy and time to be able to sustain numerous responses. Responding takes energy and it is important we do all we can to recover and rest to enable us to get better and tackle the underlying problems with action. Buy time and space, or trade space for time.
3. **Respond** - respond by doing many things. Go for many marginal gains and not the silver bullet. Make your response overwhelming. Be ready and able to remain at Action Stations for a sustained period – it might be a long fight.

The 3Rs work in harmony with some of the original science on stress and the human body. Claude Barnard (1813-78) argued that organisms are made up of an "interior milieu", a series of internal feedback mechanisms. Walter Cannon (1871-1945) introduced the concept of "homeostasis" – which is how the body maintains its internal equilibrium when faced with external stimuli, and how things return to normal after the event. When in a stressful situation all sorts of chemical and nervous system messages are released through the SNS (Sympathetic Nervous System), when you face a "fight or flight response". Once the threat is over, homeostasis occurs (return to equilibrium). Imagine sprinklers automatically being put on in a building fire to put out the danger. Once the fire is over, things need to be dried out and cleared up. Your body naturally wants to return to normal running levels and is designed to do so. By focusing on the 3Rs you are working with your body and giving it the best feedback, allowing early recognition, allowing itself to recover and respond appropriately, and then get all systems back to their normal levels.

For a good explanation of the workings of the 3Rs in extreme situations see Jonathan Brown's book "Stress and Success". As well as his inspiring personal journey; in his thoroughly researched and excellent book, he reviews stress in the light of how elite performers have responded. Jonathan helped me by making me see that although I was outstanding at the **Response** phase, I had a high R1xR2 error. I was poor at recognising increased stress levels and poor at recovering. I was particularly good at rushing late into response, without giving myself time to recover first. This is true of many leaders.

Further reading: Stress and Success - Fast Fixes for Turbulent Times. Jonathan Brown. 2013.

MANUAL STRUCTURE

I have crafted this manual so you can read it from the start in a linear way, and / or dip into, and / or return to, each of its components.

Part One is about understanding mental health attack. Chapter 2 looks at what is normal, it challenges the normal bell curve as well as exploring our natural responses to stress. Chapter 3 addresses 13 myths of stress and mental health, so these can be recognised and ignored to release us to effectively deal with stress. Part One ends with an approach to help you deal with the major stressors, the 'All Blacks' (Chapter 4).

Part Two contains 100 ideas and practical strategies to help you get to Action Stations. It starts with recognition, ideas to help you accept that you are under a mental health attack, and viewing it in different and new ways to help you deal with it (Chapter 5). This is followed by recovery, working on actions that give you time and space to think and rest so that you are able to stop things getting worse and put you in a position to move forward (Chapter 6). And then in Chapter 7 we look at responses that will directly help you get better.

Part Three is specifically for leaders. We start by helping the leader assess whether they themselves are in a situation of severe and sustained stress, XStress (Chapter 8). In Chapter 9 we introduce 15 actions that the leader can use to boost the mental health and bust the stress for their followers. We then look ahead to the future, and explore 4 likely disruptors to future mental health and what leaders can do about them (Chapter 10).

SUMMARY:

1. If you are under mental health attack - get to **ACTION STATIONS!**
2. Change the way you think, and take action - don't be a bystander, be an everyday **HERO.**
3. Accept that action has three phases: recognition, recovery and response - the **3Rs.**

Someone who had extremes of poor and great mental health, was a champion of action, a hero, and a master of the 3Rs was Winston Churchill.

Two of my favourite Churchill quotes are:

> "A pessimist sees the difficulty in every opportunity; an optimist sees the opportunity in every difficulty".
>
> And
>
> "Action this day!"

"Hero: Winston Churchill – a high performance leader who at times had very poor mental health. He was a master of using the 3Rs and of taking ACTION."

CHAPTER 2:
WHAT'S NORMAL?

What's normal?

According to the independent review commissioned by HM Government - October 2017:

> *"Our work has revealed that the UK is facing a mental health challenge at work that is much larger then we had thought. Not only is there a big human cost of poor mental health at work, there are also knock on impacts for society, the economy and Government. Employers are losing billions of pounds because employees are less productive, less effective, or off sick."*

Further reading: Thriving at Work: Stevenson / Farmer review of mental health and employers. Lord Dennis Stevenson and Paul Farmer. 2017.

According to Mind, and the NHS, one in four of us will experience a mental health problem during the year. Given the stigma of self diagnosis, the true figure is probably much higher.

So, at the macro level - there is recognition that there is a problem. It is also encouraging that mental health is now getting more media coverage and a higher profile in our national narrative, and many organisations are now taking this issue seriously. But at the micro/personal level, where do we start to work out what is normal? For each of us personally, how are we dealing with our own stress, mental health and performance?

At the personal level, we can identify stress being severe (high), and sustained (lasting for a long time). The combination of types of stress fall into the standard 2x2 box:

SEVERE but not sustained. (Normal)	SEVERE and SUSTAINED aka Mental Health Attack aka XStress (Normal!)
Not severe or sustained	Not severe but SUSTAINED (Normal)

For most leaders, at some point, being under sustained stress for an extended period is normal. Increasingly today, being under mental health attack is normal.

At the personal level, I would like to challenge the often cited 'normal' curve for stress, the start point for most approaches to stress management. For most of us in management or leadership positions, we will have attended courses, and programmes to deal with stress. We will have been told that some stress is 'good' (eustress) and that excessive and prolonged exposure to high levels of stress (chronic) can be bad. We will have been told about the "fight or flight" response and the chemical and physiological responses in our body; and the importance of getting rest, exercise and a good diet. We will have been shown the "Stress Curve". It follows a classical 'Bell' shape, or "normal distribution", with arousal (or stimulation) on the x-axis and performance on the y-axis. This is also called the Yerkes-Dodson curve after the psychologist who discovered it in 1908. With increased states of arousal caused by external stimuli, messages go to a part of the brain called the Thalamus. It then initiates the Cortex (another part of the brain) to change muscular movements and fires up the limbic system which regulates things like hormones, heart rate and pupil dilation. I.e. when faced with stress, your body automatically responds. So far, so good.

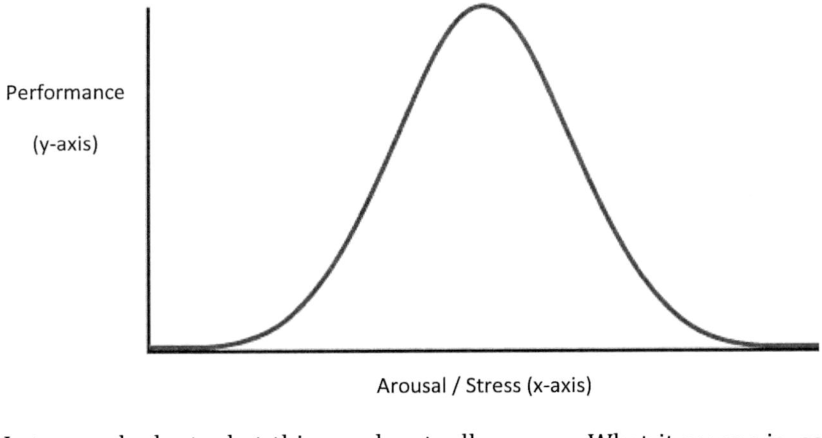

Lets now look at what this graph actually means. What it means is, as stress (x-axis) increases, performance (y-axis) rises, first slowly, then at an increasing rate up to a point where it reaches a peak. After that it falls, first quickly, then at a decreasing rate. This model originally came from stimulating responses in rats. The only problem with this – I have not found this curve to be useful in practice! My work with leaders has found that this model is not "normal" at all! In fact, to believe this model can be both misleading and dangerous! Let's look at what I think is happening.

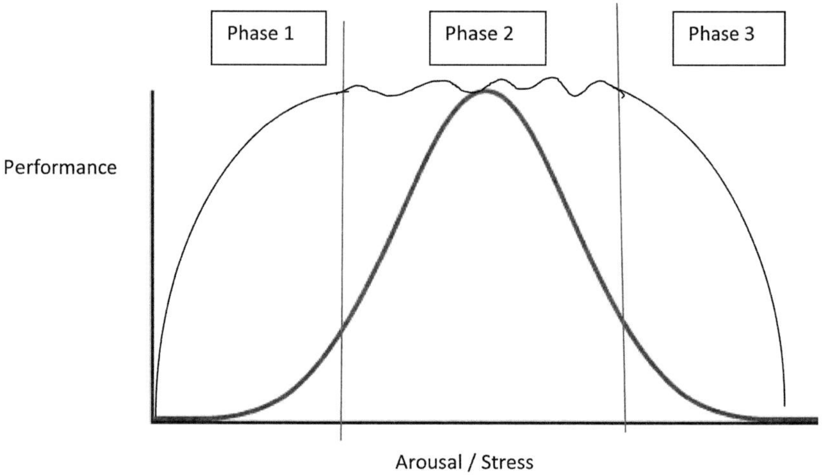

Phase 1 – most leaders do not require much stimulation / stress to get us going. In fact most entrepreneurs or high performance sports people say they need the 'buzz' to get them in the zone to perform. But this can happen pretty quickly. A head teacher walking into school, a sports team captain walking over the touch line, a business leader arriving at their factory, is usually enough to fire the adrenaline and get focus levels up. Most of us can get to high performance pretty fast. We don't need significantly increased and increasing levels of stimulation to help us do that.

The next phase, is phase 2 – this is good news. Most of us can maintain high levels of performance for quite a long time. You don't get to be leader in your field without developing some pretty good stress management skills and resilience, either explicitly or implicitly. Performance might fluctuate over the day or across days but our energy levels, drive, commitment, discipline, etc keep us performing at a high level. Most of us do not peak on a Wednesday afternoon for a short burst and then collapse. This empirical observation links in with Hans Selye's (1907-82) work on stress hormones. Three hormonal nodes, the Hypothalamus (H), the Pituitary (P) and the Adrenal cortex (HPA axis) release chemicals, creating a chain reaction resulting in Cortisol being produced. This chemical helps fight the stress and return us to homeostasis (the resting state). Along with adrenaline (epinephrine) it makes sure when faced with stress our heart rate goes up, blood pressure increases, and glucose levels are elevated. Chemicals are released to help cells communicate more rapidly with each other, and anti inflammatory and immune cells come to action stations. Selye suggested that under prolonged stress the body can, with applied techniques, re-set its stress thresholds to higher levels to help you (Heterostasis). This is certainly my experience and explains why often we can sustain high levels of stress for extended periods; however you need to watch for exhaustion, as the unusually high stress, which might be increasing, cannot be sustained forever – we need to allow homeostasis to work otherwise we could drop into phase 3.

Phase 3 is where the danger is. Because when things go wrong, they go wrong FAST and at a faster rate. This to me, partly explains why mental health is relatively harder to deal with the more mature the condition. Recovering the situation from phase 3 is very hard. Slowing down and reversing a decline is harder when you are in freefall. Phase 3 would normally be associated with absence from work, loss of confidence, medication, multiple issues, sleep disruption, or worse.

So, to conclude, we need to catch high stress earlier and make sure leaders do not fall out of phase 2 into phase 3. The challenge is to realise whether we are in the early part of phase 2 or the latter part. The 100 actions in Chapters 5 to 7 are all about how you slow down and reverse the move from phase 2 into phase 3. Realising you are in the final part of phase 2 is key to our mental health and maintaining our performance.

Talking this through with other leaders has led me to believe that not only is the traditional (normal distribution or 'rats') model wrong, the narrative that goes with it is too. In fact, it might well be possible to reduce the stress and increase the performance! What my manual is aiming to do is to enable you to re-draw the curve in phase 2 and stop you sliding onto phase 3, i.e. keep improving your level of performance without increasing the stress. The actions set out in Chapters 5 to 7 will allow you to do this through recognising, recovering and responding to the stress.

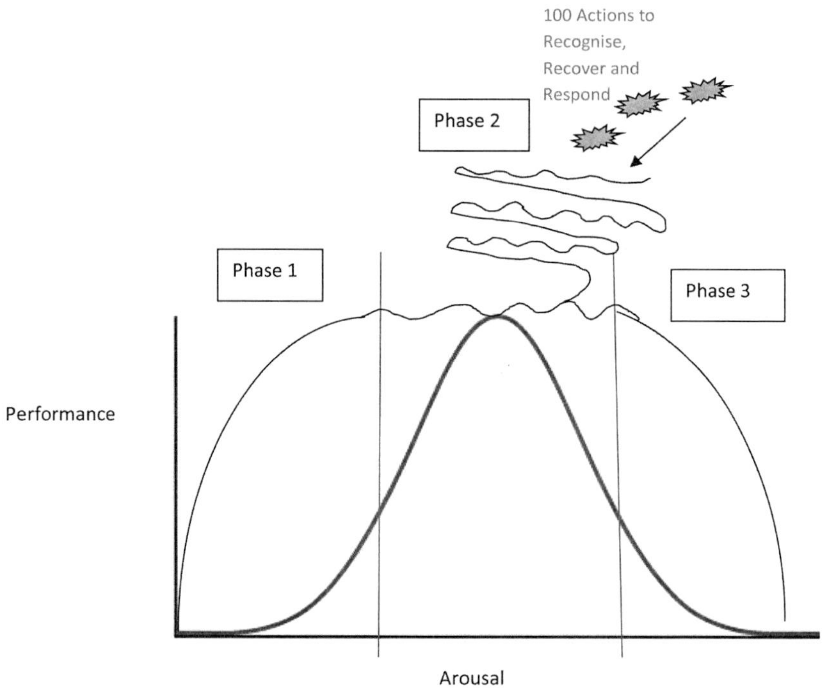

This simple graph is backed up by some science. For a full assessment of the role played by chemicals in your body a good read, if you are interested in the science, is The Science of Stress.

Further reading: The Science of Stress, what it is, why we feel it, how it affects us. Yeung, Ivkovic, and Fricchione. 2016.

If I have not lost you and you want to get into the elite/extremes of the subject, recent work on Post Traumatic Stress Disorder (PTSD) and "Allostasis" also supports this graph. Simply, that your systems are multiple, interactive, dynamic and adaptive and (after Sterling and Eyer 1988), that after extreme stress you might encounter a crash (bad); or move to a position of post traumatic growth (or anti fragility) where we are stronger as a result of the experience, you stay within phase 2 but with higher performance. If you want to be further challenged, some argue that you can learn to use stress to make you better and stronger. Some of the more progressive thinking in this space now suggests that you can reduce the negative impact of stress, and that the actions you take, particularly connecting with others and your beliefs, can transform the impact stress has on you.

Further reading: The upside of stress ... why stress is good for you (and how to get good at it). Kelly McGonigal. 2015.

For those of you who would prefer a less academic route up the mountain, here is my layman's explanation of the complex interplay between chemicals and your neurological system.

"PUGH, PUGH, BARNEY MCGREW, CUTHBERT, DIBBLE, GRUB."

This line comes from the 1967 children's TV series Trumpton, as the Fire Brigade were called into action. When we are faced with "stress" our fire sprinklers are automatically activated. If the stress is sustained, our body calls out its own fire brigade to deal with the stress (the fire). In the words of "Captain Flack" (Head of the Fire Brigade) "Right men, Action Stations!" Think of your body as a building, and the stressors creating a fire in it. As an automatic response, lots of little firemen are transported all round your body with their hoses to put out the fires (chemicals released in your body, and flood through all your systems). When the threat has gone, "heaters" automatically come on to dry out the building (your body) and return to normal (homeostasis). This is a good and perfectly natural response. However, if the fires are regular and intense, as in prolonged stress, the internal fire brigade are working overtime, which can lead them to get exhausted as they are on constant duty. This does not give the internal infrastructure time to recover and return to normal. This wear and tear, as with a building, can lead to all sorts of other physical failures in infrastructure. We can deal with stress, but only if we give ourselves time to rest and recover. If our fire brigade (our natural stress response systems) is in high and sustained use, there will certainly be a damaging impact on its capacity to respond as well as on the infrastructure (our body) that it serves.

HORMONES – CUDDLING IS GOOD (USUALLY)

There is a hormone that we all have, called Oxytocin (also called the "love hormone" or "cuddle hormone"). It is known to play an important part in reproduction, particularly in the mother-infant attachment. It is also present in men, although we tend to have more Testosterone rather than Oxytocin. It is a "feel good" hormone, and we can stimulate the release of it. Although it affects men and women in slightly different ways as our brains are wired differently, we can all trigger the release of this feel-good hormone. Many of the 100 actions in this manual, require engaging (attaching) with others. Interestingly it seems biologically women are more readily disposed to seek help from their peers, when under stress. This is certainly supported empirically with my work with leaders, we men are often slower to recognise stress, and less inclined to seek the help of others, or even talk about our stress with others. The Testosterone kicks in when we energise to "fight it", rather than seek attachment and help. And while the "fire brigade" can be automatically called out, there are things we can do to feel better by triggering the releases of more Oxytocin. Oxytocin helps to release dopamine, which stimulates our brain's pleasure centres; it lowers the release of Cortisol; increases the pain-attacking chemicals; suppresses the triggering of fight and flight neurones; and increases the release of sedative chemicals that help us return to the relaxed normal state. These hormones are automatically released in childbirth and with breastfeeding, but you can also stimulate them by the following activities. However, many of these only work if the attachment is with someone you trust or love:

Cuddling someone you love (particularly your child).
Sex (or even better "making love" with someone you love).
Enjoying a massage.
Enjoying eating.
Enjoying exercising.
Enjoying some sunshine.
Petting a dog.

So, a walk in the fresh air with someone you love and your dog, followed by a good meal, a cuddle and a night in ... sounds like a good place to start the stress fight back!

SUMMARY – WHAT'S NORMAL?

It is normal ... to be under stress.
It is normal ... to be under a lot of (severe) stress.
It is normal ... to be under a severe stress for a sustained period of time.
It is normal ... to be able to manage high levels of stress and keep performance high for a sustained period. Your body has amazing mechanisms to cope with this, and these mechanisms are chemical as well as behavioural.

But it's also normal to be close to the edge and not realise it. Your natural stress management mechanisms can get exhausted and wear out. Let's watch for this, spot it and reverse it, both for ourselves and those who follow us. If we miss this, we might slip into a fast decline, and then face a hard climb back to recovery. The earlier we catch it, the better. For the readers amongst you working at the elite end of positive mental health, the holy grail is to reduce stress and increase performance.

The key to all this is **working with** our normal natural chemical responses, and **working on** our behaviour and relationship with others.

CHAPTER 3: THE MYTHS OF STRESS AND MENTAL HEALTH

Before we turn to the 100 actions - let's deal with things that are normally said or believed but are FALSE – the myths of stress and mental health. These 13 things people might say to you, or you say to yourself, and you believe to be true. Be careful, they are not true. They can lead you down blind alleys, and at worst, can actually lead to higher stress! Let us deal with them quickly. And where you hear them in your life, challenge them. We are looking for the truth. In my experience, most people can handle the truth a lot better than they can lies, deception or deceit no matter how well meant.

Myth 1: "Stress is all about perception – just think positively".

FALSE. Perception is very important but a sole focus on simply thinking positively can be dangerous. My personal model for stress is as follows:

$$P \times D > B \times C$$

P = your perception of the situation (internal)

D = the demands of your situation provided by the environment - the stressor (external).

B = your beliefs in your confidence to respond well (internal)

C = your capability to respond (internal and external).

We feel stressed when P x D is greater than B x C i.e. when the perceived demands of the situation are greater than your believed capability to safely deal with the situation. Hence perception P (and beliefs B) are VERY important, and these CAN be changed fast. But critically D and C are also very important. If we are about to enter a week-long monsoon, perceiving it as a short shower can be unhelpful. The real power of P is to give you a realistic assessment of D.

What is often missing from the narrative, is our capability (ability, knowledge, experience, confidence, skills) to respond to situations i.e. C. So, recognise that perception is important (psychologists are right) but so is building up your response "B x C". In the modern world, D has become large for many of us due to the impact of information technology, and we also find that the time and space for C are also under attack.

That was where I was going to leave it, but some recent work has caused me to make one final adjustment to the equation. The work of McGonigal (mentioned above in Chapter 2) has shown that most people believe stress to be harmful. She explores evidence that if you change your belief to stress being HELPFUL, not only is your response to stress better, but also the long-term impact on you is better. So, to my equation I am going to add β. β is our meta belief about the impact stress will have on us; either we believe it will harm us or we believe it will help us. On the left-hand side of the equation: If $\beta > 1$, it means that we view stress as harmful to us and this scales up the threat. If $\beta < 1$, it means we view stress as HELPFUL to us, and scales down the threat to us. On the right-hand side of the equation: If $\beta > 1$, it means that we view stress as harmful to us and this scales down our capacity to respond. If $\beta < 1$, it means we view stress as HELPFUL to us, and scales up our capacity to respond.

$$\beta\,(P \times D) > (B \times C)\ 1/\beta$$

I.e. if we perceive the stressful situation to be harmful [β>1]
our perception of the situation (P) x the demands of our situation provided by the environment (D), are made BIGGER by a factor of β
AND
our beliefs in our confidence to respond well (B) x our capability to respond (C) are reduced by 1/ β

Or if we perceive the stressful situation to be HELPFUL [β<1]
our perception of the situation (P) x the demands of our situation provided by the environment (D), are made SMALLER by a factor of β

AND
our beliefs in our confidence to respond well (B) x our capability to respond (C) are increased by a factor of 1/ β

The evidence is, if we view a stressful event as an opportunity to engage and rise to the challenge, to learn and grow, and to connect with others, then we are viewing the stressor as helpful rather than harmful. The new science tells us that this helps deal with both the short and longer term consequences of stress.

Imagine giving a public presentation - something that even the most experienced managers often find "stressful". I do this a lot in my work, I enjoy it, and think I am good at it, BUT I always get a stress response every time I get to my feet ...

My hands are sweating, my heart is racing, my adrenaline is pumping - but this is because I am excited and enthused to be giving this presentation, and it is a great opportunity. This is my body's response to help me nail it and perform well.
$\beta<1$ = Helpful

As opposed to:
My hands are sweating, my heart is racing, my adrenaline is pumping - because I am petrified to be giving this presentation, and I will probably make a mess of it - I'm no good at presentations. This is my body's response telling me I am about to crash and burn.
$\beta>1$ = Harmful

Don't get too concerned with the maths or the neuroscience and chemistry behind it but there is sufficient evidence that whatever you believe about stress, you are right! If you believe stress will harm you, you are right! If you believe stress will help you, you are right! Perception is important but stress is not just about perception. The 100 Action Stations! points will give you things that you can do to not only improve P,B,C but also in β, your meta belief!

Myth 2: "Mental health is binary – either you are well or mentally ill".

FALSE. I believe mental health to be on a continuum, a spectrum. This is similar to physical health, from the seriously ill patients at one end to the super fit athletes at the other. We all have mental health. We all sit somewhere on the scale...

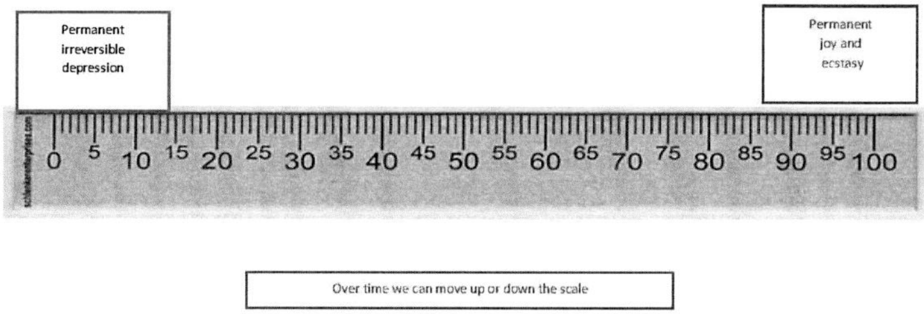

Where are you now? Mark where you believe you are currently on the rule. If you are near zero – please seek medical advice. This manual is for those not at the extreme, but for those who are under attack and being pushed closer towards 0. I have found it useful to ask leaders to place themselves in one of the following six categories. The category you place yourself in might, of course, change over time.

	-3	-2	-1	+1	+2	+3
Title:	Serious condition	Not well / struggling to cope	Normal range		Very fit/ well for an amateur	Elite fitness/ wellness for an athlete
Normal parlance:	Mental Health condition	Mental health problem	Distress - stress		Eustress	In the elite zone
Performance features:	Long term off work.	Short term off work.	Acceptable / average performance.		Good performance	Elite performance
Typical dispostion:	Can't face work.	Hate going in.	Good days and bad.		Liking it	Loving it
Typical medication:	On multiple medications.	On medication.	Self medicate with non presciption drugs (tablets, coffee, alcohol, etc).		None (other than sport or hobbies).	None (extreme engagement in sport or hobbies).
Your score on the continum?	0-20	21-40	41-60		61-80	81-100
Where do you score?						

Having scored yourself – you might want to validate this with your spouse or partner, work colleague or peer. Find out what score they would give themselves and give you? How would your followers score you and themselves? If we plotted the whole population – where would they sit? My assessment is that we have too many of us scoring less than 40, the pass mark in national health. What is the cost of this to ourselves, our families, our businesses, our communities and our nation? Mental health is not binary. We all have it, and it changes over time. We can help ourselves move up the spectrum.

Myth 3: "I need to find an answer".

FALSE. There might not be AN answer. The evidence is that often people suffer in situations of multiple conditions. For example, you might be suffering from extreme anxiety, lack of sleep, financial worries, a back problem, poor diet and an eating intolerance or disorder. They might stimulate and aggravate each other. Very rarely does health align itself to one set of symptoms. So, there might be many answers, or none. You might even be asking the wrong questions. You might find yourself in the continuing referral trap where you are referred from one health professional to another, like 'pass the parcel', in search of AN or THE answer that might not exist. This itself can cause stress. Abandon the quest. Abandon "Why am I not sleeping?" This is a bad question. Maybe more helpful is "What things can I do today that might give me a better chance of some sleep tonight?" This is a good question.

Health professionals usually can help – but they might not be able to provide you with AN or THE answer. Outside the professionals, from whom should we take counsel? When it comes to diagnosis and the search for answers to your health please "Avoid the Fs" – they are dangerous:

Friends
Family
Fanatics
Fools
Fellow sufferers
Fingers (tapping away on our PC/Ipad/phone).

My experience is in the diagnosis and acceptance stage, engaging with the Fs is problematic, although they can help with recovery. The people who are closest to us have huge amounts of emotional baggage, and are often under stress by proxy from us. The irony is, the greater the love for us, the greater this emotional baggage is. When looking for an opinion, I am reminded what my Professor at Southampton University would say (reinforced by my experience as Non-Executive Director) ... "a good opinion is not one you necessarily agree with, but is **expert, independent and informed**". In the Google/Twitter/ Instagram and focus groups age, where everyone is expected to have an opinion on everything, it can be helpful to recognise that not all opinions are equally valid.

Good opinion = ei^2

e = expert – do they know what they are talking about?
i = independent - are they giving it to you without any financial, emotional or professional (ego) baggage or vested interest in the outcome?
i = informed – do they understand your particular context?

In a world dominated by the web and social media, where a million opinions are easy to find, be careful; a good opinion is often hard to find. There might be one, many, or no answers. Seek out opinions that are expert, independent and informed, and this will then help lead you to answers.

Myth 4: "It won't get worse".

NOT HELPFUL. It might, and often does get worse! I have found giving yourself false hope and then crashing when it does not realise, is problematic. Research into Prisoners of War has shown that it is the realists who survive, not the optimists. Be optimistic about your ultimate outcome but realistic about your immediate position. The reality is that we do not know what tomorrow will bring. If today is bad, tomorrow might be worse ... or the same ... or better. If you can accept these positions and tomorrow turns out not to be worse, then already you are ahead of the game. You also de-couple your wishes from outcomes, which can be healthy. A really healthy situation is where you say to yourself, with belief, when looking at your immediate path ahead ...

It might get a bit worse - which is OK.
It might be the same - which is OK.
or it might be a bit better - which is also OK.

Now let's throw in 2 extreme scenarios -
It might be a lot worse - which is OK,
or it might be a lot better - which is also OK.

Think of something that is on your mind now. Create these outcomes in your mind, and get to 'OK' with each of them.

Outcome	What does this look like in a future time frame (tomorrow?)	Is this OK? (can I deal with this). Say to yourself
It might get a bit worse		This is OK
It might be the same		This is OK
It might get a bit better		This is OK
It might be a lot worse		This is OK
It might be a lot better		This is OK

Don't fool yourself with "it won't get worse" - it might. Accept all five as possible outcomes, but at the same time, I have one eye on the horizon, which is: in the long run the aim is to get better.

Myth 5: "Nobody else is suffering".

FALSE. Stress, wellbeing and mental health are the number one challenge of our time. 40% of us admit to having a mental health challenge. Given the stigma of admittance, the true figure is probably much higher. In fact, if you are suffering, you are probably "normal". We are all suffering to a greater or lesser extent (Buddhists are right on this one!). We are all somewhere on the mental health continuum.

Myth 6: "I can cope on my own - I don't need any help".

MAYBE, MAYBE NOT. This one is often heard amongst successful leaders. But the evidence is that others can help with the problem, solution and speed of recovery. It should be treated like any other management problem. Even if you can do it on your own, it is usually faster and better to work with others on it. A rule of thumb is to take the letter "I" out of your narrative: this speeds recovery!

Myth 7: "Just think about the worst-case scenario".

MIGHT NOT BE HELPFUL. I have found this to work in some situations where the worst is not too bad. In these situations, you can accept the worst and then work back from there. But if the worst is very bad, and often it appears to us that it is, then it can make you even worse using this technique, and trigger even more stress. Only think about the worst-case scenario if it helps and motivates you, if not dump it immediately.

Myth 8: "I only have 'this' amount of time".

FALSE. YOU DON'T. You almost certainly have much more, or much less time, than you think. Most of us are really bad at estimating how much time things take. Things usually take much longer than we think or can be done much faster. 99% of the cash flow forecasts for start-up businesses that I have seen, over-estimate the speed that sales will come in. Building new teams of people likewise. When managers and leaders keep a time diary they often find that how they spend their time is totally different from how they planned to spend their time; and how they thought they spent their time. Time management is an 'old school' technique which is much under-rated. The reality is that not all of us are excellent at managing time, and time budgeting - estimating how long things will take, is one of the hardest skills. This skill is going to become more important, and more difficult to master as the information age accelerates.

With this in mind, turning to your health, when you say "I must get better by Easter" ... this does not help. "I'm better this week than I was last week" – does help. You might get much better in a few days or it might take a few months - we don't really know. The key thing is not to slow the process down by poor thinking. Finally utilising our subconscious and developing some of the 100 techniques can actually create you extra time. More of this later. Every time you, your supporters or the experts put a time line on something, challenge it; you have probably got much more or much less time than that! Don't be fooled by the time magician.

Myth 9: "It's all about me"

FALSE. NOT HELPFUL. Some of the best leaders do personalise the journey. This drives them on and galvanises support as they make themselves vulnerable, and this creates an almost magnetic force to pull followers to them. When things start to go wrong, over-personalising is often dangerous. Taking all the responsibility for a situation which only you can influence often adds to the downward spiral for us as individuals. Over-personalising usually makes the situation worse, especially for leaders. Move the focus away from you and the past, onto action and the future. Look-in on your situation from afar, depersonalise and treat it as a management challenge. It is about you, but don't make you the focus of your thinking.

Myth 10: "If this happens it will be really bad, and I will not be able to respond".

NOT HELPFUL. Most of the things we worry about end up not happening. Popular psychology tells us that 85% of what people worry about never happens! If it does happen it is often not as bad as we think; the impact on us is smaller or our ability to cope with it is larger than we thought. This sort of thinking wastes energy and actually makes you feel worse. There are often too many variables and 'known unknowns' let alone the 'unknown unknowns'. Drop them! My dad used to tell me:

"It probably won't happen;
And if it does, it probably won't be as bad as you think;
And even if it is, you probably have the ability to cope much better than you think".

Myth 11: "I just need to stop".

FALSE. Doing nothing is hard and might be even worse than continuing. 'I can't cope with my job so I will walk away', might be the right thing, but it might create an unemployed situation which is as bad or worse. After saying that, stopping might help, and quitting, or removing yourself from a harmful context could be a good move. My rule here is: stopping A and starting B can be a good move. Stopping A and doing nothing is often a bad move. Doing nothing brings its own stress, and this is often significant. Many people have their holidays disrupted, when they "stop" physically, and their mind continues to race. You could find yourself in a position where you are thinking about your problem yet unable to move it forward, which is actually worse than being in the front line and being able to deal with it. So, consider stopping - but if you do, replace it with a new challenge or context.

Myth 12: "Mental health is about being mentally ill".

FALSE. A better way to approach this is to think of mental health as we do physical health, and think of 'fitness' not illness. Can we think of 'mental fitness'? If so, we will need to change the way we think about our mental situation. As a wise civil servant once told me, partially tongue in cheek, to be successful in the service you need to accept that all Government Departments are named the opposite to their real focus, and what they spend their timing doing. Inspired by "Sir Humphrey":

Department	*Real focus*
Health	Illness.
Education	Lack of literacy, lack of numeracy
Defence	Projecting power and waging war
Legal	Law breakers (Criminals)

Transport	Traffic jams, and lateness i.e. lack of transport
Treasury	Spending no money
Foreign Office	Our national interest
Cabinet	Prime Minister's interest, not that of the cabinet
Work & Pensions	Unemployment & benefits.

Add more of your own....?

Using this contrarian approach, rather than thinking about health from an illness perspective, can we think about health from a fitness perceptive? How do we get excellent mental health? If it's on a continuum, we can just as easily talk about grades of fitness as we can grade of illness. Let's think like an athlete not a patient. There is a lot of literature on physical fitness. If we are serious about preparing for stress, we might learn from sports science. Athletes prepare and train to develop their fitness in a number of sub domains. These differ amongst experts and sports scientists but broadly most would agree they could be classified something like: Power / Strength; Speed; Mobility / Agility; and Stamina. Let's borrow this classification. Many entrepreneurs and leaders I have worked with have very high levels of mental fitness. Like with physical fitness, training, exercise and practice can improve your fitness in all these areas.

Mental power / strength = the size of the positive thoughts you have.
Mental speed = how many positive thoughts do you have per minute?
Mental mobility / agility = the speed, per minute, that you turn negative thoughts into positive.
Mental stamina = the length of period you can sustain negative thoughts and deal with them.

	Meaning in mental health	How fit are you? Your score /10?
Mental power / strength	The size of the positive thoughts you have.	
Mental speed	How many positive thoughts do you have per minute?	
Mental mobility / agility	The speed, per minute, that you turn negative thoughts into positive.	
Mental stamina	The length of period you can sustain negative thoughts and deal with them.	

Myth 13: "Mental health is about having a mental health condition".

FALSE. A mental health condition is a label the experts give someone who has sustained poor mental health and is exhibiting specific physical / behavioural symptoms. So, you will not have a mental health condition unless you are in a very extreme situation. But your health is affected by your thinking, and we should all be aware, where in phase 2 we are, and make sure we don't slide into phase 3 of the mental health curve. Being under mental health attack is normal. A mental health condition is often located in phase 3 of the normal curve.

Treating people with mental health conditions (scoring sub 20s out of 100) is of course important, as is treating all people with extreme physical ill health. But it is not for this manual, and much has already been written about this. This manual addresses how to deal with a worsening mental health situation and then how we maintain our mental health in the positive zone. How do we stop ourselves sliding down the scale and then move up the scale, so we are closer to 100 than 0? If we are to do our bit to support the wonderful NHS, it must surely start with all of us trying to get our scores as high as we can i.e. preventative health deterioration?

We might think about mental health as a ladder, and not just as a condition, each higher rung representing better states of mental health.

The Mental Health ladder - it is not just the bottom rung.

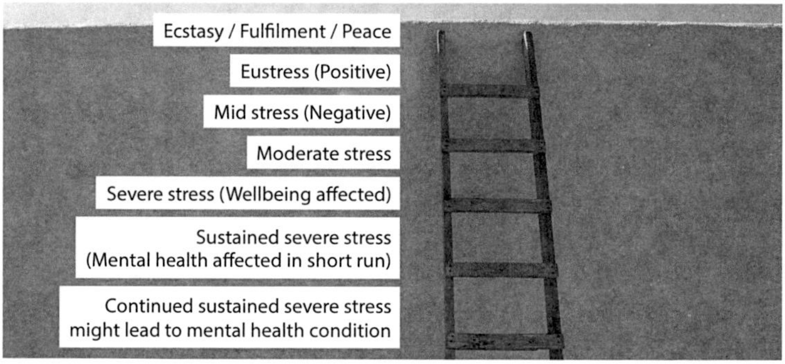

What is your current position on the ladder? Your position on the ladder is a temporary one – you can move up!

SUMMARY

So far, I have found 13 myths of stress and mental health. If you see any of these myths, challenge them. Most of us cling onto these negative myths, and this baggage slows us down and stops us moving forward. Most of us can move fast if we realise we are in a critical situation and are able to release ourselves from the things that hold us back.

My granddad and his generation faced a lot of stress between 1939 and 1945! I remember being introduced by my grandad to some of his mates (veterans) at a coffee morning, in the 1970s. Most of those present had landed on Sword Beach in Normandy, on or just after D-day 1944. As a young boy, I was very excited and a bit in awe of this group of heroes as

I saw them. I remember asking them what they thought and felt about landing on Sword Beach. A mental health question? At the time, I did not fully appreciate their answer. It was tinged with military humour, as they all laughed together in their response to me. Over the years, I have often reflected on the power and humility of their answer. It was ... "What did we think and feel when we landed on the D-day beach ...

"GET OFF THIS B***** BEACH FAST!"

If your mental health is under attack, Chapters 5-7 have actions you can take. But first dump any of the 13 mental health myths that are your baggage, and then you will be able to get off the illness beach fast.

Summary of the 13 Myths of Stress and Mental Health

	Myth - drop this baggage to help you get off the beach fast.	Challenge	Good news / Deal with:
1	*"Stress is all about perception – just think positively".*	Perception is important but not the whole story.	Lots of things help, including thinking positively. Build up your capability to respond (C) as well as your perception (P) and beliefs (B). All this is overshadowed by whether you believe stress is helpful or harmful (β).
2	*"Mental health is binary – either you are well or mentally ill"*	No. It is on a spectrum / continuum.	We are all somewhere on it and move up and down over time.
3	*"I need to find <u>an</u> answer".*	Not necessarily.	Drop it. Might be many answers or none. Change the question. Use independent, expert and informed opinion to help you get to answers.
4	*"It won't get worse".*	It might, and often does.	Accept it. It's OK.
5	*"Nobody else is suffering".*	They are.	We all are to varying degrees. Learn from those who deal with it well.

6	*"I can cope on my own - I don't need any help".*	Maybe.	But, we can all benefit from help.
7	*"Just think about the worst-case scenario".*	Might not be helpful.	Drop it.
8	*"I only have 'this' amount of time".*	You don't.	You almost certainly have much more or much less (both are good).
9	*"It's all about me".*	Yes, it is about you, but not all. And not helpful.	Drop it.
10	*"If this happens it will be really bad, and I will not be able to respond".*	It might happen. And it might be bad. But it might not happen. And even if it does, it might not be bad. And even if it is, you might be able to respond well.	Drop it.
11	*"I just need to stop".*	Maybe.	Be careful of false promises. Doing nothing can be stressful. Re focus and redeploy instead.
12	*"Mental health is about being mentally ill".*	No.	Same as physical health. Be the fit athlete, not the patient.
13	*"Mental health is about having a mental health condition".*	Not necessarily.	Is an extreme version, but wherever we are, we can move up the ladder.

CHAPTER 4: DEALING WITH THE "ALL BLACKS"

Most of us can handle one or two major issues in our life at the same time. You don't get to be a leader or high performer if you cannot. But sometimes, and it seems to be happening more frequently for leaders, many issues come at once. Psychiatrists Holmes and Rahe identified 43 events which could lead to illness in life. They gave each factor a score so they could predict the chance of illness. Their top 5 were: death of a spouse (score 100), divorce (score 73), marital separation (65), imprisonment (63), death of a close family member (63) and so on. You add up your scores and the higher the number, the greater the chance of illness.

Further reading: Social Readjustment Rating Scale. Holmes and Rahe. 1967.

It has now been 50 years since this work was published. Many of the items are still relevant. However, there are two notable omissions that I have found in my work with leaders today.

Firstly, the scores that your partner/spouse gives - can affect you. This is particularly the case now where most households have two wage earners, and often both are stressed. If you are living with someone, their mental health affects you, and vice versa. This is often overlooked when we deal with work-related stress. If you are not living with someone, then this can bring its own mental health challenges. The burdens on the generation aged 40-65, where most of today's leaders sit, seem greater than ever. The pressures on us all to make time for a life outside work are greater, our children are staying financially dependent for longer, and our parents are living longer, often requiring care.

The second omission, which compounds the first, is the role of information technology and social media on our lives. With many leaders reaching leadership roles at an earlier age, this is set to accelerate. Information technology has broken down the separation between home/personal and work so we are now more likely to let work stress seep into our home/personal lives, or vice versa, as work has gone into the virtual 24/7 world. 'Work' used to be a **place** we went to, it is now **something** we do.

Thankfully deaths and imprisonment are rare, but what I have found is that many of us are dealing with many items further down the list. Things like: a major client leaving your business; the quantity of important work cannot fit into the time available; more and more being asked from us on fewer resources; major reinvestment or re-organisation involving redundancies; major changes in role. Our multiple work-driven challenges are landing on us at the same time as the demands on us at home are growing.

Making a list of all the main stressors can be helpful. You might like to put action points against each, or rank them, or share with your partner / spouse. Making the list is usually more cathartic than you think it will be.

Action: Make a list of the big stressors (for you and your partner) and rank them.

Big stressors for me?	Big stressors for my partner?	How important are they?	What action can we take?

Today it is common for leaders to be handling more than one major issue in work (two or three are not uncommon) and more than one major issue outside work (again two or three are not uncommon). I have developed an approach which I have used in my mentoring work. First, make a list of all these major issues – dump them on a page – now tally the number. How many do you have? Try to separate the normal (business as usual stressors) from the really big ones.

I call these big major challenges and stressors coming towards us ... "All Blacks". This is named after the New Zealand Rugby Team who wear the black shirt. How many "All Blacks" (major stressors) do you face?

For some of my mentees, I have found it useful to explore the following story. Imagine you are an England Rugby full back, playing at Twickenham, against the New Zealand "All Blacks", the most successful international rugby nation. It's the last minute of the game which is finely poised. An "All black" breaks through, and you are the last line of defence. It is a 'one-on-one'. Do you back yourself to take him/her down? Most (English!) leaders I put this to say YES. Why? *It is Twickenham in the last minute against the "All Blacks" – this is my moment. I am the best in my position in England. I am fit, focused, brave, capable, and have prepared for this moment mentally and physically. And although he has a Fern on his shirt I have a Rose on mine – he's/she's going down!*

Now imagine the same scenario but this time two "All Blacks" coming – it's now a '2 on 1', against you. Would you back yourself to stop the try? In my research group of leaders, some say yes, some say no, some are not sure. The more confident and bullish say yes – *we watch the hips for 'roll' – and in the perfectly timed moment we decide whether the offload is coming (when the ball is passed), and we hurl ourselves towards one of the two, to take that player out. If our reading of the game is right, we land on them the split second they receive the ball. If we can't read the pass, our chances are 50/50 – we take one out and hope he/she is the one with the ball.*

What about three "All Blacks" coming at you – it's now a '3 on 1'? Pretty much all the leaders I have asked say that the position is hopeless and there is nothing that can be done to stop the try.

In a sporting sense this concept has different names such as elimination, or OVERLOAD. I.e. the attacking side are trying to create a situation where their options, capability and firepower overwhelm the defence. Whatever decisions are taken by the defenders, the game will be played out, leading to victory for the attacker.

So the question is – how many "All Blacks" are you facing? In the business of mental health, if you have two or more "All Blacks", you might be in a stress OVERLOAD position, which is not good. The perfect mental health attack for your enemy, is to set you against too many 'All Blacks', creating an overload, and where all plays lead to a deterioration in your mental health.

So what are the common "All Blacks"? Research among today's leaders and high performers has revealed this list:

COMMON "ALL BLACKS" ARE BASED ON NELSONSPIRIT WORK (2018) WITH LEADERS...

1. Death and bereavement.
2. Illness of a close family member or self.
3. Concern over the wellbeing of a child or parent.
4. Concern over the wellbeing of spouse/partner.
5. Concern over the wellbeing of self.
6. Relationship issues with a child or parent.
7. Relationship issues with a spouse/partner.
8. You or partner having an affair.
9. Risk of losing your job/major contract.
10. Risk of legal action against you.
11. Risk of your reputation/good name/character being attacked.
12. Business merger, takeover, sale, cessation or change in ownership.
13. Business cash flow difficulties.
14. Personal cash flow difficulties.
15. Worry about not having enough money in the medium or longer term.
16. Concern over relationship with boss.
17. Having to deal with more and more work on less and less resource.
18. Culture at work has changed for the worse – not like it used to be.

19. Concern with the relationship with a major customer or supplier.
20. Relationship with a powerful individual at work (bullying or power games).
21. Comparison with others – I/we are falling behind, socially or financially.
22. Non-acceptance or lack of recognition by your peers.
23. Mid-life crisis – a search for meaning and purpose.
24. Life event cross road – e.g. child birth or children leaving the nest.
25. Concern that you are trapped on medication and can't get off it.
26. Addictive behaviours (drugs, alcohol, sex, medication).
27. Long term unhappiness with life.
28. Concern that you are always tired.
29. Sleep problems.
30. Boredom – not enough challenge.
31. Your spouse/partner/girlfriend/boyfriend scoring 2 or more of the above.
32. Your spouse/partner/girlfriend/boyfriend scoring 4 or more of the above.

This is not an exhaustive list. You might well have an 'All Black' not on this list which is specific to your situation. However, this list might be a useful starting point. Do you face any of these?

Let us revisit this list and mark against each whether they are a major stressor for you. How many 'All Blacks' do you face?

"ALL BLACK" CHECKLIST

1	Death and bereavement.	
2	Illness of a close family member or self.	
3	Concern over the wellbeing of a child or parent.	
4	Concern over the wellbeing of spouse/partner.	
5	Concern over the wellbeing of self.	
6	Relationship issues with a child or parent.	
7	Relationship issues with a spouse/partner.	

8	You or partner having an affair.	
9	Risk of losing your job/major contract.	
10	Risk of legal action against you.	
11	Risk of your reputation/good name/character being attacked.	
12	Business merger, takeover, sale, cessation or change in ownership.	
13	Business cash flow difficulties.	
14	Personal cash flow difficulties.	
15	Worry about not having enough money in the medium or longer term.	
16	Concern over relationship with boss.	
17	Having to deal with more and more work on less and less resource.	
18	Culture at work has changed for the worse – not like it used to be.	
19	Concern with the relationship with a major customer or supplier.	
20	Relationship with a powerful individual at work (bullying or power games).	
21	Comparison with others – I/we are falling behind, socially or financially.	
22	Non-acceptance or lack of recognition by your peers.	
23	Mid-life crisis – a search for meaning and purpose.	
24	Life event cross road – e.g. child birth or children leaving the nest.	
25	Concern that you are trapped on medication and can't get off it.	
26	Addictive behaviours (drugs, alcohol, sex, medication).	
27	Long term unhappiness with life.	
28	Concern that you are always tired.	
29	Sleep problems.	
30	Boredom – not enough challenge.	
31	Your spouse/partner/girlfriend/boyfriend scoring 2 or more of the above.	
32	Your spouse/partner/girlfriend/boyfriend scoring 4 or more of the above	
	Others ... not mentioned above	

	Others ... not mentioned above	
	Others ... not mentioned above	
	How many do you face?	

Are you in overload, i.e. facing more than 2? (3 or more)?

The research evidence is that it is common for leaders and high performers to be facing 4+ "All Blacks" at once! So, if you have scored 4 or more don't panic - this is normal. But obviously not ideal. Assume you are the smiley face....

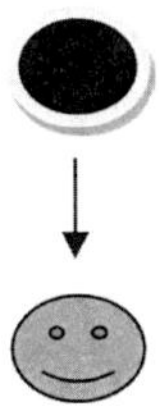

One "All Black" - this is OK

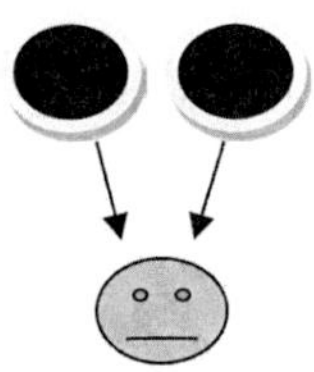

Two "All Blacks" - this might be OK

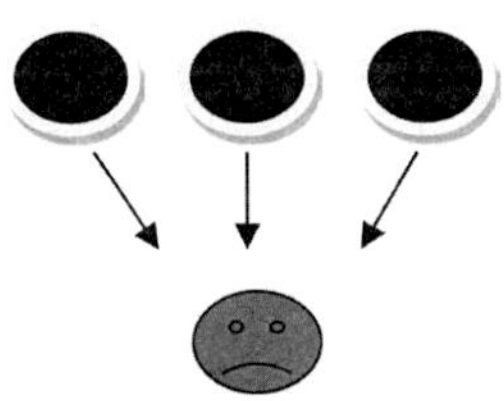

Three or more "All Blacks" - this is <u>not</u> OK

Remember most of us can handle one or maybe two of these at any one time. If we get to 3 or more, then we most certainly will have overload. No matter how fit you are physically, or how strong your mind, you will lose this play as the forces stacked against you are so great. Remember overload is where all plays lead to you losing. And losing is your mental health getting worse.

So how do we win? How to we deal with overload? How do we make sure mental health increases and doesn't decrease? If you have more than two "All Blacks", the first thing to do is to recognise that this is where you are. What action can you then take to deal with this? The leaders I have posed this question to, have identified two main solutions:

- STRATEGY ONE: As I can take down one 'All Black', I will deal with them one at a time. The interesting thing is that while at first you might think they are all coming at you at once, usually not all will have an impact in the short term. So, it is usually possible to arrange the 'All Blacks' into some sort of time sequence. One or more you might be able to pick off and push back to be dealt with later. So, arrange your problems in a sequence and deal with them one at a time. Assuming four "All Blacks":

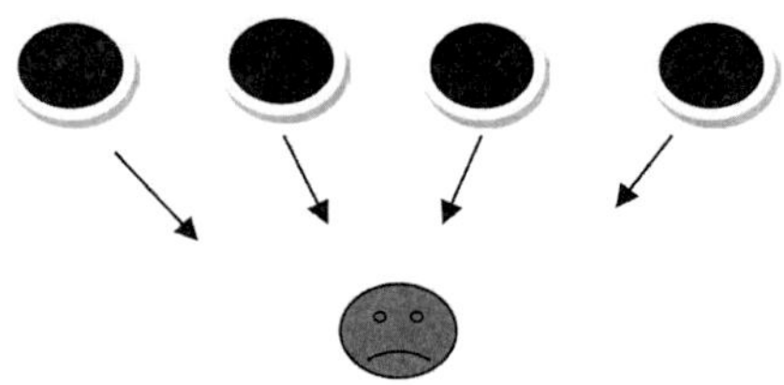

Change to:

- STRATEGY TWO: Get a few team mates on the pitch to help you deal with the overload and change the odds. In practice, it is often not possible to arrange for all the big stressors to be dealt with one at a time, so usually we will need to engage with both strategies. But there is some brilliant news ... most of us know a lot more people than we think, and most of these would be delighted and honoured to help us - IF WE ASK THEM! One of my big lessons from my own experience was so many people said - "*Why did you not mention this to me - I would have helped?*"

  Change to:

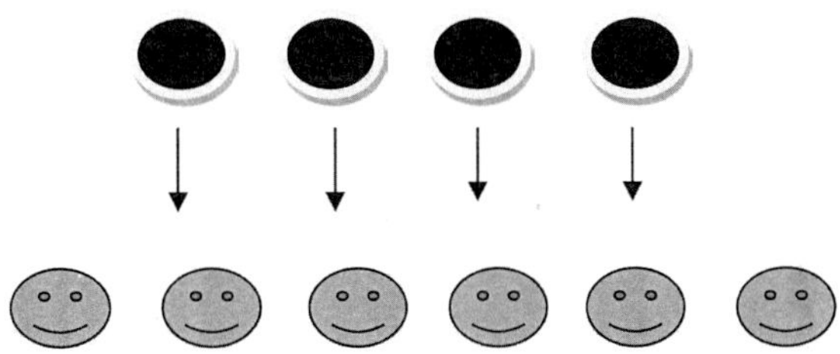

The uncomfortable truth is that many leaders are playing a team game with most of their own team on the bench! Get them off the bench and on the pitch!

If you have 4 "All Blacks" - call up 5 people to help you. Now it's 4 of them vs. 6 of you; no overload and you win.

One way of getting this moving is to share your "All black" list with your friends or mentor and ask them to help you deal with your "All Blacks". Then later maybe you can help them deal with their list?

FUTURE LEADERS

The world is changing, and my research with leaders has also shown that AGE (or stage in life journey), matters in relation to what things stress you.

Working with Future Leaders has shown that young people have some 'All Black' issues on the main list that are not pertinent to them, and others which are pertinent are missing from the adult list. Working alongside some great charities such as the YMCA, The Broadland District

Council Youth Advisory Board (YAB), and The Nelsonspirit Future Leaders Crew, has helped us identify "All Blacks" of particular relevance to Future Leaders. We found that while some issues affect us all, there are differences across the generations. The Future Leaders work has mainly been with older teenagers. This is still work-in-progress, but here is what we have so far:

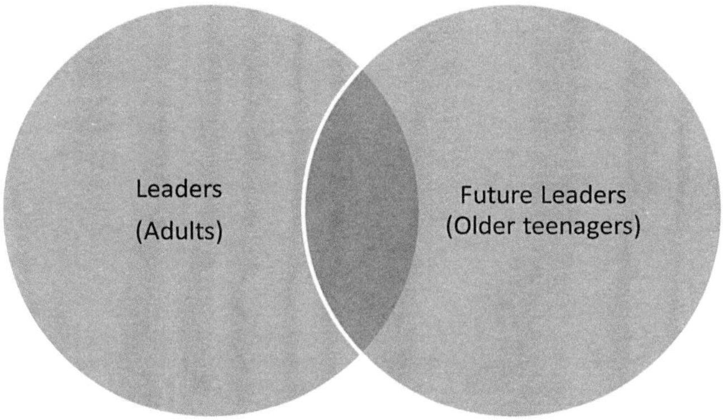

We find that some 'All Blacks' are unique to adults, some are pertinent to both groups, and some are unique to older teenagers.

SOME 'ALL BLACKS' COMMON FOR FUTURE LEADERS / TEENAGERS

1. Choosing what you want to do for the rest of your life – university/job/gap year/apprenticeship (what are you going to do when you grow up?)
2. GCSE and A-level exams and revision, coursework, and homework.
3. Time management - deadlines to hand in important school work or UCAS form.
4. Time management - getting over committed, either through too many opportunities or wanting to help/please parents, teachers.
5. Meeting University grade requirements.
6. Pressure of living up to expectations, from parents, teachers, peers or self.
7. Relationships with friends including jealousy of others, and disputes with friends.
8. Social media - body confidence and body image.

9. Social media - too much time spent online (potential addiction to platforms, Snapchat, Twitter etc).
10. Self esteem and personal confidence.
11. "FoMO" – Fear of Missing Out.
12. Negative stereotyping of young people.
13. Fear of the world (terrorism, global warming, war, Brexit, housing, economy).
14. Your partner/girlfriend/boyfriend scoring 2 or more of the above
15. Your partner/girlfriend/boyfriend scoring 4 or more of the above.

Again, this is only a starting point. It is likely that individual responses might differ across age, gender, social class, and income levels. But it might be useful to give this list to your children or grandchildren, if only to start a conversation. Then see how you can help them with their list, and how they can help you with your list.

FUTURE LEADERS "ALL BLACK" CHECKLIST

1	Choosing what you want to do for the rest of your life – university/job/gap year/apprenticeship ... what are you going to do when you grow up?	
2	GCSE and A-level exams and revision, coursework, and homework.	
3	Time management - deadlines to hand in important school work or UCAS form.	
4	Time management - getting over committed, either through too many opportunities or wanting to help/please parents, teachers.	
5	Meeting University grade requirements.	
6	Pressure of living up to expectations, from parents, teachers, peers or self.	
7	Relationships with friends including jealousy of others, and disputes with friends.	
8	Social media - body confidence and body image.	
9	Social media - too much time spent on line (potential addiction to platforms, Snapchat, twitter etc).	
10	Self esteem and personal confidence.	

11	"FoMO" – Fear of Missing Out.	
12	Negative stereotyping of young people.	
13	Fear of the world (terrorism, global warming, war, Brexit, housing, economy).	
14	Your spouse/partner/girlfriend/boyfriend scoring 2 or more of the above.	
15	Your spouse/partner/girlfriend/boyfriend scoring 4 or more of the above.	
16	Any from the main (adult) list	
	Others ... not mentioned above	
	Others ... not mentioned above	
	Others ... not mentioned above	
	How many do you face?	

Are you in overload, i.e. facing more than 2? (3 or more).

I recognise my own bias, as a patriotic Englishman interested in sport. But before moving on I would like to pay tribute to the real 'All Black' leadership and performance philosophy. As I borrow their "shirt" to make a point, I respect their achievements and their spirit. High performance sport teams can teach us much about managing mental health. None more so than the New Zealand Rugby Team.

Further reading: Legacy - what the All Blacks can teach us about the business of life. James Kerr. 2013.

From this excellent book: *"Successful leaders look beyond their own field to discover new approaches, learn best practices and push the margins. Then they pass on what they have learned".*

And from the Maori:
From listening comes knowledge;
From knowledge comes understanding;
From understanding comes wisdom;
From wisdom comes wellbeing.

Listen to yourself and your friends. Identify your "All Blacks", and see if you can use some of this spirit to lead you back to wellness.

Action: Dealing with the "All Blacks" – identify how many "All Blacks" you face. Are you in "overload"? If so, deal with them one at a time and / or get some team mates on the pitch to help you.

"Heroes: How many "All Blacks" can you manage?"

PART TWO:
100 WAYS TO DEAL WITH STRESS AND IMPROVE PERFORMANCE

SCRAMBLE!

The 100 actions in Chapters 5 to 7 are designed to help you get to "Action Stations" ...

Pre-flight safety briefing:

a) All 100 actions work. But certain ones may not work for you, or not be effective in your situation, or you might not like them. In fact, sharing the first draft of the manual has shown me that different people warm to very different actions. Choose the ones that take your fancy and deploy them. A checklist is available at the start of each chapter and at the back of the manual.

b) It is a numbers game. Do not just do a few and expect a result. You will need to do many over a sustained period to get a result.

c) Use as a complement to advice provided from health professionals.

Because of a) and b) I have resisted the temptation to streamline the number of actions, and give you my best 10 etc. You need to find the shortcuts, I cannot give them to you. I also present them in random order, so those of you that like a hierarchical structure might be a bit outside your comfort zone! View it as a 'dog fight'. You never know when the next opportunity might appear as you read through. Some of the 100 actions are designed to help you deal with stress, improve mental health and improve performance by Recognition (Chapter 5), or by Recovery (Chapter 6), or by Responding (Chapter 7). So here we go, 100 ways to get you to ACTION STATIONS!

CHAPTER 5: ACTION STATIONS! – RECOGNISE

Recognise - Recover - Respond

Recognition – accepting that you are under a mental health attack and viewing it in different and new ways, to help you deal with it.

Chapter summary - in case you prefer to dip in ...

		Hero:	
1	Listen to yourself - "Google your soundtrack". Lay down a positive soundtrack today.		
2	Identify your support network, and bring them to alert.		
3	Form a round table of your Knights, based around character and capability.	King Arthur	
4	Catch it, Kill it, Cook it, Eat it. Adopt the mindset of a survivalist.	Bear Grylls	
5	You probably have more, or less time, than you think. Both are good.		
6	Accept that you might need to take unprecedented action.	Queen Boudicca	
7	Games can be, and often are, won in "Fergie time".	Alex Ferguson	
8	Go on a Mental Health First Aid course, or speak with someone who has, or read up on it, or simply adopt a First Aid mindset to your mental health.		
9	Engage Enemy More Closely - if we are to get better health and seize victory, we need to take personal responsibility and get close to the problems.	Admiral Nelson	
10	Refer yourself to the doctor. Then ask for a referral. Do it now, but see it as part of the overall picture not THE answer.		
11	Two heads are better than one - find a health partner.	Rolls Royce	

12	Give yourself good intent. Something like "I intend to get better". Each day, work towards getting better.	GB Ladies Hockey	
13	Reframe 'losing and pain', as 'winning and fun'. Start with trying to have a bit more fun, redefine winning, and then start to believe you can win.		
14	Think freely, deal with the evidence of what is today, not what might be tomorrow.	Thomas Paine	
15	Live in the present, not in the past or the future. Focus on enjoying and performing in what you are doing today - leave yesterday and tomorrow alone.		
16	Actively use the most powerful two letter word, OK, to deal with acceptance, reflection and action.		
17	Reducing difference reduces stress, but so does being comfortable with difference.		
18	Accept that rationality and irrationality are both imposters. When it comes to your health, use both to move you forward.		
19	From fixed to growth mindset - challenge yourself every day - am I limiting myself by adopting a fixed mindset? Would it be better to adopt a growth mindset on this?		
20	Recognise that to have a "chimp" as your inner voice is normal. Accept that he/she is not the same as you, and keep him/her in their box.		
21	Syndromitus - use the label to bring focus, don't let a mental health condition define you.		
22	Be realistic, up to a point.		
23	Be delusional, up to a point.		
24	Recognise that you have "one pie's worth of energy per day" - cut it and eat it wisely.		
25	Minimise the "give away" and "take away" of your time and energy.		
26	Accept that even though you may be weak and feeble in body, you can be strong in spirit.	Elizabeth I	
27	Go to the source of the river, find out where it began and this will help you understand where you are and what you need to do.	Jack Reynolds	

1. Listen to yourself – "Google your soundtrack".

   Imagine if everything you have ever said was recorded onto a soundtrack, i.e. every word you have ever spoken was captured on a CD/digital recording. This would be the soundtrack of your life. It would be possible then, just like a Google 'bot', to analyse this soundtrack and classify sentences and statements into POSITIVE and NEGATIVE. Now reflect on the past week, on everything you have said. Classify them into positive and negative. People with good mental health, score mainly positive. People with excellent mental health have nearly all positive. We all know people who are great to be around because they are so positive, they exude positive energy. In fact, we tend to attract people around us whose narrative is like ours. If we have a positive sound track, other positive people are attracted to us. If we have a negative soundtrack we attract negative people. Positive people with a positive narrative make you feel better. Negative people with a negative narrative, make you feel worse. We control the soundtrack of our future. Today's soundtrack has not yet been recorded. So, it's still possible to lay down a positive soundtrack for today. Become mindful of your own soundtrack, and surround yourself with people with a positive soundtrack. If someone is being negative, challenge them, say "To help me, I am trying to surround myself with people who have a positive soundtrack", it will make you and they feel better. Some of the great entrepreneurs I have worked with have a very positive soundtrack, and this is both infectious and engaging. One for me is my sister Beverly who has a very positive soundtrack, and we always look forward to being with her.

   Action: Listen to yourself – "Google your soundtrack". Reflect on how positive it is. Commit to laying down a soundtrack today that is more positive and surround yourself with people who have positive soundtracks. Challenge people when they are not positive enough.

2. Identify your support network, and bring them to alert.

   We all know a lot more people than we think. Most of these people will help you, if you ask them. Most of us are not good at asking for help. Here is a simple exercise ...

   The stick man in the centre of the page resembles you.

   Now draw in all the people you know and label them. Once complete you could repeat the exercise with how "close" they are to you, measured by the length of the line, the shorter the line the closer they are to you. Most of us know some pretty amazing people. How do we get them engaged supporting our health? How do you get key people closer to you? How do you engage better with your support network? You are not alone. Together this group of people could help you move fast to recovery. Identify a couple who would be very helpful and contact them today. Now re-draw with your key contacts.

   Action: Identify your support network, and bring them to alert. Bring them to Action Stations!

3. Form a round table.

   Once you have identified your support network you might like to think about the 'few' that you will bring closer to you. Your most trusted Knights.

King Arthur was a sixth century king who led Britain against the Saxon invaders. While much has been written about Arthur and his court, most of it is cloaked in folklore, myth and magic. Much is debated, and even his existence is disputed. However, many of the stories have a romantic appeal. One story is the moment when the warrior king meets with his nobles. They are squabbling around a table, arguing about their self-importance and who should sit next to the king. Should it be the bravest? The richest? The strongest? Arthur takes off his gauntlet and with his bare fist smashes the table so hard it disintegrates into many pieces. There is silence. Arthur announces that there will be a new table … a round table, and he will sit at the table as first amongst equals. Also he will be inviting men from far and distant kingdoms to sit with him as his Knights. The test for knighthood will be one of capability and character, and not of favour of the king. Capability would be proved on the battlefield but character (or chivalry) would be tested by what you do and why you do it, off the battlefield. In these acts Arthur is credited with affirming the Knights' code, something which has influenced many organizations and laws over the last 1400 years, including codifying of the responsibilities of Directors into UK law. Many branding and HR professionals are now talking about business managers and leaders having their own "personal board". Arthur's inspiration is to teach us that to be a great leader (king, prime minister, managing director) you need to surround yourself with a great table of knights. The best round tables, be they boards or cabinets, are councils of equals built upon firm principles. It is useful to reflect that *charisma* might bring people to the table, but it will be *character and capability*, that will deliver the ultimate results. In the business of improving your health your best friends might not be your best knights. When you are not feeling well, your friends will often tell you what they think you want to hear. A knight will tell you the truth. Who do you have around your table? And by what code do you conduct the business of improving your health?

Action: Form a round table of your closest Knights based on character and capability.

"Heroes of the past: King Arthur and his Knights".

4. Catch it, Kill it, Cook it, Eat it.

   The topic of survival / SAS is very popular on the book shelves and on TV. The starting point for 'survival' is to recognise that you are in a survival situation. Research shows that many who get into trouble do not think they are in a survival situation. The same is true for mental health. Many who end up off work and on multiple medications recognised too late that they were in a tight spot. Early recognition helps. You have more time to deploy actions, more energy, and recovery is easier the less severe the stress. Here are some general rules on survival that I believe are applicable to mental health:

   - Recognition that you are not in the mode of 'normal living'. You are in a survival situation. Normal rules don't apply, and you will have to adopt a new way of thinking to survive.
   - It requires a change in attitude <u>and</u> deployment of survival skills. When it comes to mental health, the action points in this manual can help you with both. This latter point is crucial. In order to survive you have to do stuff, and the right stuff, not just think positively.
   - Surviving also requires a focus on the basics of wellbeing – protection, location, water, food. All survivalists know that they need to 'catch it, kill it, cook it and eat it' and they need to 'get a fire on'. These basic but critical actions are where

their attention should be on. This clarity of purpose can be very helpful.

A modern hero and someone who exemplifies great mental health in hostile environments is Bear Grylls. You cannot watch Bear without noticing that he uses all his physical, mental, emotional, and spiritual energies to improve his situation. He does it all with a smile.

Action: Catch it, Kill it, Cook it, Eat it: adopt the mindset of a survivalist – change your attitude, deploy skills, focus. Be like Bear.

"Hero: Bear Grylls, be like Bear".

5. You have more, or less time, than you think.

   Generally, we are not very good at estimating how long things take. When it comes to our health most of us are very poor at putting realistic timelines on our situation. The evidence is, that we usually have much MORE time than we think we do. Or, we have much LESS time. For example, "I expect to be better and return to work within a month", is not helpful. It might take 6 months or 6 days. Putting an artificial time line on something, and predicting, can often induce more stress! Every time someone, including yourself, says you have X amount of time, challenge it. You usually have much more, or much less. Accepting this helps. Make time your friend, not your enemy. Also on a simple practical level, sometimes externally set deadlines can be moved with the agreement of those you report to.

Action: Accept that you probably have more, or less time, than you think. Both are good.

6. Queen Boudicca - accept that you might need to take unprecedented action.

   Boudicca (Boadicea) was Queen of the Iceni, a tribe mainly based in Norfolk who were the thorn in the side of the imperialist Roman aggressors. Boudicca led her peaceful tribe in revolt to defeat the Romans in Colchester, London and St Albans. In fact, they were the only tribe from ancient Britain to defeat the Romans in Battle. The stealing of her land, the rape of her daughters, and her personal whipping resulted in her people rising up. Unprecedented circumstances demand the courage for an unprecedented response. Boudicca is arguably Britain's first national hero. She led her armies of Norfolk men and women farmers to defeat the greatest military force the world had ever seen. How much of the Boudicca's story is myth is hard to tell, but when the stakes were raised to a level beyond the norm, she united her people to follow her into action. She weaved land, pride, external threat, honour, and personal and tribal insult into the leadership mix.

   Boudicca's inspiration is to teach us that unprecedented situations require unprecedented action. We need the wisdom to decide whether we are at that moment, and if we are, to have the courage to take the action that it demands. With mental health, most of us fail to recognise that the situation has significantly and substantively changed, and that we are under critical attack. The early signs are usually things like disrupted sleep, body pains, being grumpy, loss or increase of appetite etc. Most of us ignore these signs and as the situation builds, continue to behave in a 'business as usual' way. If we accept that the attack is unprecedented, we take the first step in getting ourselves ready to make an unprecedented response. I have found that even the realisation that you are under excessive stress or mental health attack helps in taking the first steps.

Action: Be like Queen Boudicca - accept that you might need to take unprecedented action.

"Hero of the past: Queen Boudicca – take unprecedented action".

7. Games can be, and often are, won in "Fergie time".

   'Fergie time' is named after the legendary Manchester United Football Club Manager Sir Alex Ferguson. Opponents would claim referees would give Manchester United too much extra time (after the 90 mins) when they played at Old Trafford, Manchester's home ground. In addition, Man Utd. had a reputation, and habit, of scoring in the injury time or "Fergie time", after the 90mins. If you have had a stress situation for a long period and it has shown no improvement, don't panic or give up. One goal in Fergie time can win the game for you. The key thing about Fergie Time is that the Manchester United players expected to score after 90 mins, and this belief spurred them on. We often don't know the length of the health game. It might not end for a long time, and you don't know where you are in the game. Believe you will get better, believe in Fergie time.

   Action: Accept that games can be, and often are, won in "Fergie time".

"Hero: Sir Alex – Believe in 'Fergie Time'".

8. Mental Health First Aid.

   There are an emerging number of Mental Health First Aid courses you can attend. I like the concept of "First Aid". It is action-based, and helps you focus on what you can do immediately to stop the situation getting worse, bring comfort to the patient, and then send for help which will bring benefit in the longer term. Apply the concept and principles of First Aid to your own mental health. You could consider going on a course or, if pressed for time, research their material and distil the lessons for yourself. A good start point might be Mental Health First Aid (MHFA) CIC.

   Further reading: www.mhfaengland.org

   Action – attend a Mental Health First Aid course, or speak with someone who has, or read up on it, or simply adopt a First Aid mindset to your mental health.

9. Engage the enemy more closely.

   Many will be familiar with Admiral Lord Nelson's signal at Trafalgar: "England expects that every man will do his duty". But this signal was flown only once. Nelson's favourite signal, which he would typically raise as his fleet approached the action, was "*Engage the enemy more closely*". As part of his leadership style, and arguably a contributor to his success, was his encouragement of his captains to get very close to the enemy. His view was that this was the best way to secure victory. In business, as in life, defining the enemy is critical. In the boardroom if we define "the enemy" as "falling margins" we need to get closer to understanding the underlying numbers. How much of the problem is due to falling sales (with a semi-fixed overhead)? Sales mix? Changing sales prices? Discounts? Poorer buying? Stock movement? Wages? Productivity? How are all these numbers moving by the month? By the week? Basing an action plan around a close analysis of the numbers that make up the problem can be extremely motivational. Of course, the analysis alone is not sufficient. The next step is to engage the hearts and minds of those who need to change their behaviour in order to get the numbers moving in the right direction.

Nelson's inspiration is to teach us that if we desire victory, then we need to get close to our problem. We must have the courage to face the problem, to face the dangers of the battle, and maybe even put our reputation on the line to fix the problem. Of course, it is much easier to comment from afar ... blame the economy, the government, the competition, or the staff, rather than getting stuck in and sorting it out.

When it comes to mental health, get close to your health issue. You also might like to think carefully about what is the enemy, and make sure you don't mis-define it in error. The end product of Nelson's battle philosophy was all out Victory. Adopt this mindset, define your victory. He also took courageous personal responsibility for the outcome. Don't leave the outcome to 'The Admiralty' (health professionals), seize responsibility yourself. With your "health enemies", engage the enemy more closely, and then you might seize victory, from the jaws of defeat.

From Nelson *"I am of the opinion that the boldest measures are the safest".*

Action: Engage the enemy more closely – if we are to get better health and seize victory, we need to take personal responsibility and get close to the problems.

"Hero of the past - Admiral Nelson.
'Engage the enemy more closely'."

10. Refer yourself to the doctor. Then ask for a referral.

    We have a wonderful thing in Britain called the National Health Service. But many of us do not refer ourselves to our GP. This problem is particularly acute for we men! And particularly a problem for leaders! So, if you are a male leader ...

    There are all sorts of reasons why we don't self-refer. Maybe it's ego. Maybe it's not seeing mental health the same as physical health. Maybe it's because we don't want to waste people's time. Maybe it's because we equate GPs with illness. Maybe we see others as needier. However, it is my experience that most leaders do not ask for help from their GP until the situation has got extreme, and the solution then usually involves drugs, and time off work. Go early, and see what your GP can do. Also ask for a referral. GPs tell us that a third of the patients they see have a significant mental health element to their condition. Your GP might not have the answer, if in fact, there is **an** answer, but they might be able to signpost you to others who can help.

    Action: Refer yourself to the doctor. Ask for a referral. Do it now, but see it as part of the overall picture, not THE answer.

11. Two heads are better than one.

    There can be great comfort in working with someone else who is in the same health situation as you, but different in personality and background to you.

In 1904 Charles Stewart Rolls took the train from London to Manchester to meet Fredrick Henry Royce. He was accompanied by his friend Edmunds, who had suggested Mr Rolls and Mr Royce meet. Rolls was born in Berkeley Square to a rich London family. He was educated at Eton and Cambridge, owning the first ever automobile in Cambridge. Despite this, he was a little different from the typical aristocrat: he was careful with money, sparing with food, and modest with alcohol; and his "hands on" approach to engineering got him the nickname "Dirty Rolls". At the time of the first meeting with Royce, Rolls was selling cars. He wanted to sell the best cars in the world, and was frustrated that this meant he had to stock only foreign cars.

Royce by contrast came from a poor family. His father had died in a poorhouse. Royce was brought up with money worries and had many jobs to make ends meet. While working he took evening classes and eventually qualified in mechanical and electrical engineering. He then set up his own small business trading as an electrical engineer. After some success, they hit hard times and Royce collapsed through overwork. While resting, he drove his first car. He loved it, but was disappointed with its reliability. He thought he could do better. On his return his reluctant board allowed him to design, build, and try to sell 3 cars! According to Edmunds' account, Rolls and Royce "took to each other at first sight" and eagerly discussed the prospects of the emerging automobile industry. Interestingly Edmunds, the man who brought them together, was referred to as the "umpire" in that he acted as arbiter to draft the agreement and make sure it was fair for both parties. In return he was given shares in the highly risky and innovative new venture to be called Rolls-Royce! Despite (because of) their different backgrounds, they made a formidable team.

If you can, find someone you get on with, even though your backgrounds might be very different. If you have a common interest, it might be more productive and healthier, if you team up. Two heads are better than one. You have someone to encourage you, to compare notes with, and to support you who knows what you are going through. Make sure they are a positive person.

Action: Two heads are better than one – find a health partner.

"Heroes of the past. Two heads – Charles Rolls, Henry Royce."

12. Is our "intent good"?

    All high-performance sports people know, you cannot determine the result of a game but you can control things like your attitude, work rate, focus etc. In sport, we cannot guarantee that we will win the game, but we can commit to having this as our intent. Likewise, with health. We cannot determine that we will get better today or tomorrow, but we can have a strategic intent of "getting better". Interestingly, knowing the commanders' strategic intent is one of the bedrocks of modern military thinking which underpins 'mission command', an approach to leadership used by many modern armies. Some days, some parts of the game, and some parts of a battle, you will feel as though you are not winning and you are going backwards, but if your intent is good, in the long term you will make progress.

    The GB Women's Hockey team of 2016 was brilliantly led by Kate Richardson Walsh. A team built on friendship, spirit and underpinned by hard work and with strong mental health. They went on to win Gold in the Rio Games. Dr Hannah Macleod, a key member of the playing squad, highlights that one of the team's secrets was to establish a culture where the focus was on 'good intent'. We all make mistakes but with good individual and collective INTENT – we can achieve gold.

Action: give yourself a good intent. Something like "I intend to get better". Each day, work towards getting better.

13. Reframe 'losing and pain', as 'winning and fun'.

    If you believe you are winning – you are right. If you believe you are losing, you are right. Psychologists tell us that BELIEF is key to our behaviours. Knowledge of military history and sport tells us that most battles are finely balanced, and the gap between winning and losing is a small one. So, if you are feeling that you are losing and you are in pain, reframe or redefine. Start to tell yourself that you are winning. From personal experience this often starts with telling yourself that you are enjoying the fight. If you can convince yourself that this is true then you can start winning. The key thing here is that you must believe it. While I have found that this technique does not work in all situations, often a defeat or massacre is a loss, no matter how you dress it up, if you can have a bit more fun, it's amazing how many times you start to feel as though you are beginning to win, and the stress can fall away.

    Action: Reframe 'losing and pain', as 'winning and fun'. Start with trying to have a bit more fun, redefine winning, and then start to believe you can win.

14. Think freely - deal with evidence.

    A powerful technique to deal with health is to just look at the facts. We all allow possibilities of the future to cloud our judgement about health. Often too worried about tomorrow, we let that affect how we feel today. When my mind starts to wander away from evidence I often refer back to Thomas Paine.

    Thomas Paine was born in 1737 and was quite a character. He was an author, pamphleteer, corset maker, customs official, privateer, shopkeeper, inventor, phrasemaker, school teacher, small businessman, bridge designer, journalist, intellectual, radical thinker, propagandist, and revolutionary. In his time he was regarded as a prophet and hero in both France and America and an enemy of the state in Britain. He was a founding father of the United States, where he wrote the best-selling work of the 18th century in America. He is credited with communicating the independence cause to the American people to rally them against the British. And in Britain he laid the foundations to some of the socialist thinking in the centuries to follow. He was regarded by the British establishment as a treasonous troublemaker. He challenged the thinking of pretty much everybody in power, threatening the power base of the three great empires of the day. Not bad for a small businessman and manufacturer of ladies' underwear!

It's impossible to summarise the three great life works of a complex man in one sentence ... but here goes ... *Common Sense* ('America should be free from Britain – fuelling the American revolution'); *The Rights of Man* ('men should be free to decide their affairs not the establishment – inspiring the French in their revolution'); *The Age of Reason* ('free thinking – opinions should be formed on the basis of science, logic and reason and should not be influenced by authority, tradition, dogma or religious practice'). He is largely omitted from the historical memory of all three countries.

Paine's inspiration is to remind us that things move fast when we are can THINK FREELY, and then use simple words to inspire people to act. Deal with the facts of what IS today rather than what MIGHT BE tomorrow. The most successful business leaders can release themselves from these constraints and blend their judgement with instinct to see a way forward, and then communicate this to their staff. When it comes to our health, it helps to think freely. Ask the experts for the facts and then apply independent inquiry and logic; free from bias, conventional wisdom, popular culture, prejudice, sectarianism, and tradition.

From Paine: *"The real man smiles in trouble, gathers strength from distress, and grows brave by reflection".*

Action: Think freely, deal with evidence of what is today, not what might be tomorrow.

"Hero of the past: Thomas Paine –
think freely, after establishing the facts, base your
thinking on science, logic and reason".

15. Live in the present, not the past or the future.

    Enjoyment can come from looking back or anticipating what is about to come, but most of our 'feel good' emotions come from what we experience in the moment. Likewise, with negativity. To dwell on what has gone wrong or might go wrong, is bad for us. Not only does it not help, it actually makes us feel worse in the moment. Living in the past or the future, if it's bad, actually ruins the present as well. If yesterday was bad, why ruin today by dwelling on it? This is important in health conditions that vary. Tomorrow might be as bad, or even worse, but let's not make today bad simply by thinking, or worse talking, about yesterday or tomorrow.

    Yesterday, today, tomorrow poem (Anon)
    There are two days in every week about which we should not worry,
    Two days which should be kept free of fear and apprehension.
    One of these days is YESTERDAY, With its mistakes and cares,
    Its faults and blunders, Its aches and pains.
    YESTERDAY has passed forever beyond our control.

    All the money in the world cannot bring back YESTERDAY.
    We cannot undo a single act we performed;

We cannot erase a single word we said.
YESTERDAY is gone.

The other day we should not worry about is TOMORROW
With its possible adversities, its burdens, its larger promise.
TOMORROW is also beyond our immediate control.

TOMORROW, the sun will rise, Either in splendor or behind a mask of clouds,
But it will rise. Until it does, we have no stake in TOMORROW
For it is as yet unborn.

This leaves only one day – TODAY.
Any man can fight the battles of just one day.
It is only when you and I add the burdens of those two awful eternities
– YESTERDAY and TOMORROW – That we break down.

It is not the experience of TODAY that drives men mad.
It is remorse or bitterness for something which happened YESTERDAY
And the dread of what TOMORROW may bring.

Let us, therefore, live but ONE day at a time.

Action: Live in the present, not in the past or the future. Focus on enjoying and performing in what you are doing today – leave yesterday and tomorrow alone.

16. The most powerful 2 letter word – OK.

When my dad was informed he had terminal cancer, I asked him how he had responded to being told this by the nursing staff. He said that he had said "OK"! On first reaction, I was a little disappointed, as my dad always had wise words in a crisis. Then he reached for his pencil and piece of paper and started to make a list – at the top of it he wrote "ACTION". I asked him why he had responded in this way? He said that, first, you need to accept where you are. And then combine this with a determination to do all you can to take positive action to move forward. 'OK' is the only word in the English language which encompasses both acceptance, a moment of reflection, and a willingness to act. I say OK a lot. Interestingly I am told by my friends in marketing that OK is the most widely used word in the world.

Action: Actively use the most powerful two letter word, OK, to deal with acceptance, reflection and action.

17. Be comfortable with difference.

    One application of the OK concept is to be 'comfortable with difference'.

    Stress increases with difference. If our health situation is different to what we expect, or what it was, or what we hope for, this causes stress. Most people who have poor health worry about their health, which makes it worse. Accepting that the situation is different from what you want, which is not the same as accepting that it is permanent, can help.

    Action: Reducing difference reduces stress, but so does being comfortable with difference.

18. Rational Economic Man and Behavioural Economics.

    When I was younger, I enjoyed the study of Economics. Economics is based on a few fundamental assumptions. One is that of "rational economic man" i.e. consumers and producers behave rationally when they make economic and financial decisions. This is of course nonsense. We are all influenced by emotions, and today more than ever, the business world is dominated by brands, seducing us to consume using all sorts of clever techniques. In effect, seducing us to behave less rationally. For example it is not rational to pay £50 for a T-shirt, bought in a shop that looks like a nightclub so dark that you can't even see the product label, when a T-shirt of similar quality, but without the label, is available two minutes' walk away for £5. But many people regularly buy brands in this way. Although I personally refuse to pay £50 for a T shirt! In recent times an emerging and interesting branch of Economics has emerged called Behavioural Economics which seeks to explain consumer behaviour where apparent irrationality is the norm. Even number 10 (Downing Street) has accepted that applying some of the understanding of irrational behaviours of the public might help us as a nation. David Halpern's book explores the Nudge Unit at the centre of government.

Further reading: Inside the Nudge Unit: how small changes can make a big difference. David Halpern. 2016.

People do and say the strangest things, and understanding human behaviour is a life study. When you are ill you might start to behave more irrationally. Furthermore, those around you can start to behave more irrationally too. I have found that work related stress is often caused by the irrational behaviour of others. I have also often given myself comfort when working with entrepreneurs, by accepting that I might be surrounded by mad men! If we accept that others will not behave rationally i.e. we expect them to behave irrationally, this can help. So, it might help to accept that rationality is holding us back and to understand that things are often irrational.

But it also might help if we are viewing things too irrationally to pull them back, to look at them more rationally! To escape the whirlwind of emotion and irrationality, if you are stressed, go back to 'O' (GCSE) level Economics, go back to rationality. Assume the world is not dominated by quasi-monopolistic brands. Act based on the fundamentals of price and quantity. We know rational economic man does not exist but we pretend he does to help us understand the workings of the economy. We cannot separate emotion from health but if we can take out much of the emotion from our assessment and try to behave with complete rationality, this might help.

Just like defeat and victory, rationality and irrationality are both imposters, as Kipling said, treat them both the same. Where are you on the rationality – irrationally spectrum? Would it help to move more to the other end?

Action: Accept that rationality and irrationality are both imposters. When it comes to your health, use both to move you forward.

19. From fixed to "growth mindset".

In a seminal piece of psychological work Carol Dweck distinguishes between a fixed mind set and a growth mind set.

Further reading: Mindset: Changing the Way You Think to Fulfil Your Potential. Carol Dweck. 2017

In a fixed mindset we make limiting assumptions about ourselves and the world around us, which are often not true. This limits, or caps our performance. High performance leaders usually have a growth mindset. They do not burden their thinking with what is not possible but instead learn from each stage of the journey which spurs them on to higher levels of performance and opportunity. If you are off work with stress, putting a time line on when you will return to work is an example of fixed mind set. Doing something each day to move you forward so that you feel better each week, working towards a day at some point when you might be able to return to work, is a growth mind set. Guess what ... the growth mind set people get better faster.

Action: From fixed to "growth mind set" – challenge yourself every day – am I limiting myself by adopting a fixed mind set? Would it be better to adopt a growth mind set on this?

20. Recognise that you are not the "chimp".

Inside our head we all have a voice that talks to us to sow doubt, worry and insecurity. Psychiatrist Steve Peters in his book The Chimp Paradox calls this phenomenon "The Chimp". Steve's work with GB cycling is an interesting read on how to deal with this inner voice and how it can be used to propel people to high performance and not hold us back. A full read of his book is worthwhile, but I picked up these three things which have helped me:

- *To have a chimp (inner voice) running around in our head is normal.* I believe the stronger the leader the louder and more active is their chimp.
- *You are not the chimp* – by separating the inner voice from me – has helped.
- *Learn to control the chimp's behaviour by keeping him in his box* – Nicki (my wife) would often have to help me put him back in his box, so I stopped thinking bad thoughts about situations. I have found he gets out of his box the most when I am not at work, and unless you control this, it can ruin your home life, sleep and personal relationships.

Further reading: The Chimp Paradox: The Mind Management Programme to Help You Achieve Success, Confidence and Happiness. Steve Peters. 2012

Action: Recognise that to have a "chimp" as your inner voice is normal. Accept that he/she is not the same as you, and keep them in their box.

21. Syndromitus - don't let mental health define you.

    One of the great challenges of having a mental health problem is that once you enter the formal health care system a quest begins to define your syndrome or condition. This might in fact involve multiple referrals. The focus of the narrative then becomes defining the condition, explaining the condition, living with the condition, meeting experts who help with the condition; assessing the risk of the condition. In fact, if you are not careful your whole life can get dominated by an endless stream of appointments and a long narrative about 'the condition'. Getting ready for the appointments, travelling to and from, debriefing from etc. Just because you are under mental health attack you will not necessarily have a mental health condition, but some of you might. Nicki my wife did. It can be helpful by recognising it formally, it gives focus to the formal medical support that can be deployed to help. But there is a danger that the condition begins to take over your identity.

    In the worst case, your life can become defined by your condition and it can limit and explain your behaviour. It can be better to think of yourself as perfectly normal and temporarily going through a health issue which is part of where you are now, and which you will recover from; as opposed to someone who is permanently defined by and dominated by their condition. Alternatively, we can re-frame how we view our situation completely. Inspiration can be found from our Para Olympians who define themselves as high performance athletes who have overcome incredible challenges in their life journey. I was lucky enough last year to see Alfie Hewett win his wheelchair tennis match at Wimbledon. During a fabulous and entertaining game, I realised half way through that I was watching *very able athletes play wheelchair tennis at a world class standard*, not *disabled athletes in wheelchairs playing tennis*. There is a difference. The former is inspirational, the latter is limiting. We should take inspiration from the leadership of our Para Olympians.

Action: Syndromitus - if you have a condition, use the label to bring focus, but don't let a mental health condition define you.

22. Be realistic, up to a point.

    Don't deal in false hope, be realistic. This is particularly helpful when it comes to expectations from attending meetings with health professionals, and time scales for recovery. Assume interventions will produce very little or nothing, then tick off the positives after the meeting. Assume you might not return to work full time in the near future, and settle for each day working towards better health so that at some point in the long term you will be able to return. Realism does not mean dwelling on the worst case. When an expert says "most people with this condition will never be able to do X" we hear "most people including me who have this condition will never be able to do X". This is too much realism. Realism means accepting the worst case, best case and all points in between. Some realism is good, but don't be too realistic.

    Action: Be realistic, up to a point.

23. Be delusional, up to a point.

    After making the point about realism, sometimes it can help to delude yourself. High levels of delusion are a common feature amongst entrepreneurs. They either don't see, or consciously do not accept the risks that things might go wrong with a project. They proceed with deluded optimism and courage which sees them through. An over focus on realism, particularly if you are facing multiple health challenges, can sometimes trigger a downward spiral to even worse health. So, in some cases a little delusion can help. A few years ago, after an operation to remove cancer, and as I lay in hospital on the day of the operation, I asked how long it would be before I could get back playing hockey? I was told, "*the realistic time-scale for recovery to play competitive hockey is 12 weeks*". My response was that this was far too long. I asked myself and the professionals what could I do to shorten it to 4 weeks, and formed an action plan around this. In the end, I completed the recovery in 6 weeks. Rather than accepting that I would be out of sport for 3 months, each day I tried to do something to shorten the time-scale. Some delusion is good, if you are not too delusional.

Action: Be delusional, up to a point.

24. Recognise you have "one pie's worth of energy" per day.

One of the most useful time management techniques that I have learnt is when someone suggested that we only have a set amount of energy per day – "one pie's worth" of energy per day. Just like with a meat or fruit pie, that you take out of the oven. The amount of the pie is fixed, you simply have to decide how you slice it. We have a fixed amount of energy per day, our challenge is to spend it wisely. Our sleep freshly bakes a pie's worth of energy each day for us to consume. The thing about the pie analogy is that you might be able to increase or decrease the size of the pie marginally, but the big decision, is how you cut the pie, i.e. how you allocate your energy each day. Energy is actually a more useful concept than time, as we can all work longer and sleep less to 'create more time' but if we view the amount of energy we have as fixed, this can be more helpful. Energy invested on one activity cannot be used on another. Energy wasted being negative or worrying not only does not help us, it wastes this valuable resource that we could be applying to our recovery. Be on your guard for enemies and friends coming to eat slices of your pie.

Action: Recognise you have "one pie's worth of energy" per day, cut it and eat it wisely.

25. Minimise 'give away' and 'take away'.

Once you have accepted that you have only one pie's worth of energy, the next thing to address is 'give away' and 'take away'. These concepts come from our friends in the food industry. 'Give away' is the waste ingredients that are lost through inefficiency. 'Take away' is the product that leaves the factory unauthorised to the wrong people i.e. it 'walks' from the factory. In an energy or time sense, who or what do you give away time and energy to? And who steals your energy/time? Tightening up on 'give away' and 'take away' can release huge amounts of time and energy for us to invest in getting better.

Action: Minimise the 'give away' and 'take away' of your time and energy.

26. Weak and feeble – attitude and spirit count.

The year was 1588. The Spanish had assembled a great Armada of ships, ready to ferry an invasion force from the Netherlands to England. As Drake and the British Fleet made plans for the sea battles, all over the south coast militia were called to arms. On 8th August Queen Elizabeth inspected her troops at Tilbury in Essex, many of whom were unaware of the Armada's fate. The Queen left her escort at the fort and rode among her people with only six guards. She arrived wearing a silver breastplate over a white velvet dress.

She (is reputed to have) said "... Let tyrants fear, I have always so behaved myself that, under God, I have placed my chiefest strength and safeguard in the loyal hearts and goodwill of my subjects; and therefore I am come amongst you, as you see, at this time, not for my recreation and disport, but being resolved, in the midst and heat of the battle, to live and die amongst you all; to lay down for my God, and for my kingdom, and my people, my honour and my blood, even in the dust. I know I have the body but of a weak and feeble woman; but I have the heart and stomach of a king, and of a King of England too, and think foul scorn that Parma or Spain, or any prince of Europe, should dare to invade the borders of my realm; to which rather than any dishonour shall grow by me, I myself will take up arms, I myself will be your general, judge, and rewarder ..."

The imagery of the warrior queen at the front of her army earnt her a place in the hearts of the English and a place in the history books. But Elizabeth's leadership inspiration is to remind us that simple visible and unexpected acts in a time of crisis by the leader, have a disproportionately positive effect. The story also highlights that while we might be suffering stress and illness physically, our attitude and spirit can still be strong. When your mental health is poor, you often feel weak and feeble physically. But, as with Elizabeth, there is no need to be weak in spirit.

From Elizabeth: *"I have the body but of a weak and feeble woman; but I have the heart and stomach of a king".*

"Hero of the past: Elizabeth I – not so weak and feeble?"

Action: Accept that even though you may be weak and feeble in body, you can be strong in spirit.

27. Go to the source of the river – Jack who?

What is causing your ill health? If you don't get this right then you might never fully recover.

In 2016 Barcelona were crowned the football champions of La Liga in Spain, which they had won 3 of the previous 4 years. And they also won the Copa del Rey (The Spanish Cup) at the end of a season where they set the Spanish record of 39 unbeaten consecutive games in all competitions. Congratulations to Luis Enrique their manager and the 2016 team who won the treble, making them the only European club to win the treble twice, as well as being the only club ever to win 6 out 6 competitions in a single season. All this in a recent era when the Spanish national side, with many Barcelona players, won 2 European Championships 2008, 2012, and a World Cup 2010. What is their secret?

My research has indicated that there are three foundations of high performance, whether it be in business or sport: people, money and leadership.

Firstly, you need excellent people (players / staff) both on and off the field of play. The very best high performance teams are always made up of great people. Secondly, money. You need to be properly capitalised. Most teams or businesses that fail have critical weaknesses in one or both areas. Venture capitalists are wary of businesses that are poorly capitalised in terms of finance and people.

Many teams both in sport and business have both, but still fail at the elite end, in that they are short of the third ingredient: Leadership. Part of the leader's role is to instil the philosophy, values and culture of how things should be done, and Barcelona FC shine as a contemporary example of this. Sharing performance, values and purpose you become more than a team. So, what can we learn from the Barcelona way?

Barcelona's approach has been created over many years and has had many great people contributing to it. But many would argue the arrival of Johan Cruyff from The Netherlands to be the wind under the Catalan wings. Cruyff was three times winner of the Ballon d'Or; inventor of the Cruyff turn; and esteemed as Europe's greatest ever player, some say the person who made the biggest ever overall impact as a player and manager in football. As Pep Guardiola put it "Cruyff painted the chapel, and Barcelona coaches since merely restore or improve it". Guardiolas' Barcelona reached a record six champions league semi-finals and won fourteen trophies in four years. Guardiola plus Cruyff account for twenty-five trophies. Guardiola played for and was mentored by Cruyff.

Barcelona's pattern of play, is clear for a trained eye to see, but what underpins this? Although adapted by specific coaches over the years it derives from a paradigm around "time and space". It is like / derived from, the Total Football played by the Dutch national side of the early 1970s. Ajax used this approach to win three successive European cups 1971 to 1973, clocking up forty-six consecutive home wins!

Having a strong philosophy can be embedded in all aspects of a business so that those who are new or are growing up in the organisation are imbued with the values and beliefs ready for when they play in the top team. We learn best from those we respect, admire, and who show interest in us. Incidentally Messi, Iniesta and Xavi were voted the three best players in the world by FIFA, all were products of the Barcelona Academy! The academy are proponents of the tiki-taka (short passes, movement, work the ball into channels, keep possession), and this was crafted for Barcelona based on the Ajax method that Cruyff had himself experienced. Interestingly, some of Barcelona's academy players would not be tall enough to have made it into the football academies of some English Premier League clubs who still have height as a criterion!

A question that has long intrigued me is – where did Cruyff get this idea from? It turns out that he himself was mentored through the Ajax academy system and was inspired by another great Dutch coach called Rinus Michels. I then wondered who inspired Michels, and it turns out he was ... an Englishman – a flat cap wearing northerner from Manchester called Jack Reynolds, who played for teams such as Second Division Grimsby Town! Jack was Rinus's mentor and manager. Jack was not a great player, but he was a great leader. He was one of the main pioneers of total football and ended up the manager of Ajax (1915-25, 1928-40, 1945-47), which he led to eight Dutch league titles. He was also the Dutch national manager, and until 1913 was also the German National Team manager (short post for obvious reasons).

To me this shows the power of leadership mentoring. As leaders, we pass on not only our knowledge but our values and philosophy too. Many business leaders I work with give credit to an inspirational mentor who shaped their ideas and encouraged them along the way.

Like your health, the Barcelona FC story is not the story of one person. But the lesson is that you cannot fully understand Barcelona FC without understanding the source of the river. In terms of your ill health, what is the source of the river? Like the story of Jack Reynolds, a man few people know, the ultimate cause of your health problems might not be immediately obvious. Don't treat the symptoms, go back and find out what started it all, and then the solution might be clearer.

Action: Go to the source of the river – find out where it all began and this will help you understand where you are and what you need to do.

"Hero of the past: Jack Reynolds – the source of the Barcelona river".

CHAPTER 6: ACTION STATIONS! - RECOVER

Recognise - **Recover** - Respond

Recover – working on actions that give you time and space to think and rest, so that you can stop things getting worse and put you in a position to move forward.

Chapter summary - in case you prefer to dip in ...

28	Build a defence system - information is processed, and responses set in action to the point of maximum impact.	Hugh Dowding	
29	Step up diary management - plan time to allow recovery.		
30	Use the 80/20 rule to deploy resources to stress.		
31	Purpose (I aim to get better) is not enough. To get better it helps to identify what drives you on - why should you get better.	Edith Cavell	
32	Understand how much sleep you need, the impact it has on your operating capability, and work on routines to make sure you get enough.		
33	Use cap naps to "power up": 10-20 minutes will boost you.		
34	Expect the pre-dawn raid - deal with it, roll over.		
35	Identify your "stay awake issue" - and share it.		
36	Turn the kit off - between certain hours - let your phone sleep.		
37	Go for a 'walk and talk' and don't talk about 'it'.		
38	Take the 'monkey' off your back, and don't accept monkeys.		
39	Don't give away power to difficult people - take the initiative, decide in advance how you will engage with them.		

40	Don't try to enlighten the 'unconscious' - their cups are full.		
41	An engaged change is better than a rest. Step up your (displacement) activity.		
42	'Art of Action' - be clear about your intent and link this to a clear response plan; expect things not to go to plan, make decisions close to the action given the unfolding situation.		
43	Accept that you should not empower others with an expectation that they have an answer - you might be disappointed.		
44	Have a 'cobra' meeting - with others or a daily/ weekly solo, to review current position, review progress and raise morale.		
45	Control or influence - accept that you can control little, but influence a lot. Be a wise King Canute.	King Canute	
46	Cut the 'salami' - view the whole as a series of digestible chunks.		
47	Play 'one-touch' - deal with a piece of communications only once.		
48	Deploy 'relaxation techniques'. Try them and adopt the ones you enjoy.		
49	If you are a thinker - understand and live life consistent with the 'mental laws'.		
50	De-personalise your situation.		
51	Blend the best of the amateur and professional, and play your health game your way - be true to yourself.	Fred Perry	
52	Step up sport / exercise regime.		
53	Obsess about being a mental athlete, not a mental patient.		
54	Borrow models / paradigms from things that interest you, and construct your health problem within the framework of a world that interests you.		
55	Use routines to help turn yourself 'on and off'.		
56	Hobbies - On the Ball City - step up, take up, or revisit and enjoyable hobby that gets you on the move and enables you to immerse yourself for a short while in another world.		

57	Does it need doing today? If so 'Action this Day' (Churchill) and 'Complete this Day' (Wellington). Otherwise leave until tomorrow.		
58	If you are spending too much time at the fence, don't. Turn off your communications. When there, classify them as they come in. Decide which you will deal with now, and which later.		
59	Make time (10 mins) to be intimate with your partner and care for them each day.		
60	Use Project Management Methodology - use time, cost/resource, scope and risk to plan for a great recovery.		
61	From Slim - get yourself a good recovery plan, be flexible about it, and limit discussion about it.	General Bill Slim	

28. Build a defence system.

    How did Britain win the air war in 1940, in the Battle of Britain? There are many reasons – the bravery of the pilots – The Few. The technology, including the legendary Spitfires and Hurricanes, and Radar that Britain had at her disposal. But the strongest reason I believe was the superior organisation, efficiency and planning that underpinned Britain's air defence system. Created under the leadership of Hugh Dowding, a complex system of information was captured using new technologies such as radar, and old technologies, such as observation from the ground, fed back to a central processing unit, which was then processed in real time. The limited resources (aircraft and pilots) were marshalled to the point in the battle where they could have the most effect. Victory in the air in 1940 secured Britain against invasion and was one of the turning points of the Second World War.

    View your health not as a victim – someone who is being attacked and will lose, but think about building a defence system. What information do you need to feed in? How can you use all the support systems out there to feed in good information that can be a help to you? How can you then marshal your limited resources to make the biggest impact in the fight for better health? Just like in 1940, some of the solutions might involve high tech and some low tech. And just like then, the more we build in robust information management and practice, the stronger our defences are. Surround yourself with lots of early warning systems and good information, so you too can marshal your limited resources to best effect.

Further reading: The Most Dangerous Enemy: A History of The Battle of Britain. Stephen Bungay. 2000.

Action: Build a defence system – information is processed, and responses set in action to the point of maximum impact.

"Hero of the past: Lord Dowding – built the defence system that saved Britain in 1940".

29. Step up diary management.

    You can be too stressed or too ill to have the time to recover! If so, step up "diary management". This is where you are thinking about and reviewing how you spend your time and committing time to your mind and diary. Give yourself the time and space to recover. Manual diaries are better than online ones. Draw charts, diagrams and lists to help sort out your time. Sometimes it can help to build in diary management time each day to work out the unfolding priorities and what action is now relevant. One of my common observations of senior leaders is their plea for their subordinates/PA/support staff not to over-fill their diary, so they have enough thinking and planning time.

    Action: Step up diary management – plan time to allow recovery.

30. The 80/20 rule actually works!

    Anyone who has studied business or been on a management training course will be familiar with the 80/20 (Pareto) rule. It says that 80% of sales come from 20% of customers. 80% of profit comes from 20% of your products. 80% of your problems come from 20% of your staff etc. It is one of those rules of thumb connected to numbers that seems to have an uncanny knack of being right in practice.

    Now think of these:

    80% of your stress is coming from 20% of your problems.

    80% of your solutions will come from 20% of the action you take to respond.

    80% of the support you get will come from 20% of the people you ask.

    My experience is that 80/20 rule actually works. Don't waste your time. Focus and use the 80/20 rule to your advantage.

    Action: Use the 80/20 rule to deploy responses to stress.

31. Purpose is not enough.

    What is the purpose of your journey? It is to be better? Healthier? Not as ill? To return to the health you used to have? Return to better health than you used to have? A good purpose might be about moving towards wellness or being more healthier. But this alone will not make us recover.

    Edith Cavell was a nurse in the First World War. She nursed both allied and enemy wounded. She also helped allied wounded escape and was later executed by the Germans as a spy. Propaganda of her execution is said to have helped America come into the war as well as doubling British recruitment in the 8 weeks after her death in 1915. Her compassion led her to help all wounded regardless of nationality. Her patriotism led her to help the allied wounded escape from hospital, despite knowing that she was putting herself at great risk by doing so. After the war, both Belgium and France showered her with posthumous honours, and on return to England, her body was guarded by the Belgium army, and the Royal Navy. A gun carriage drew her through London to Westminster Abbey. On her return to her home city of Norwich, officers, some of whom she helped escape, carried her coffin into the Cathedral Close. She died a heroine and martyr.

On the visit of the Chaplin, on the eve of her execution, she commented "Standing as I do in view of God and Eternity, I realise that *patriotism is not enough*. I must have no hatred or bitterness towards anyone". Historians debate the precise meaning of this ... but for me it highlights a realisation that the "purpose" triangle for Edith had three sides: patriotism; care for humanity through her nursing; and her faith. She did what she did, because she had three sides of her purpose triangle, not one.

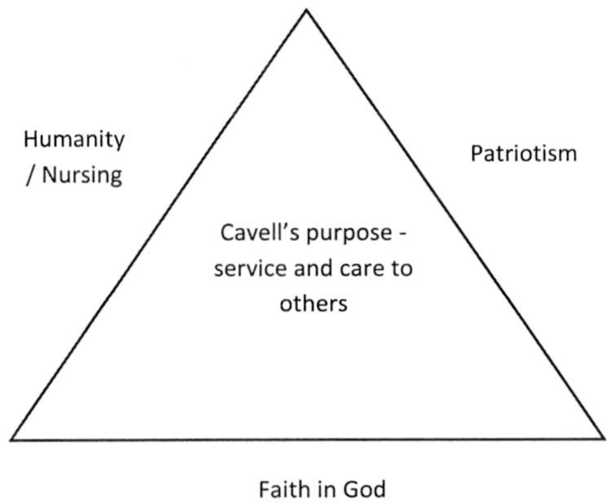

For your health, if we accept that the "purpose" is to get better – what are the 3 sides of your triangle? Put another way, what drives you to get better?

These three sides of the triangle were what drove Cavell on. What might your purpose triangle be? What drives you on? Why should you get better? You want to get better because, x, y, z?

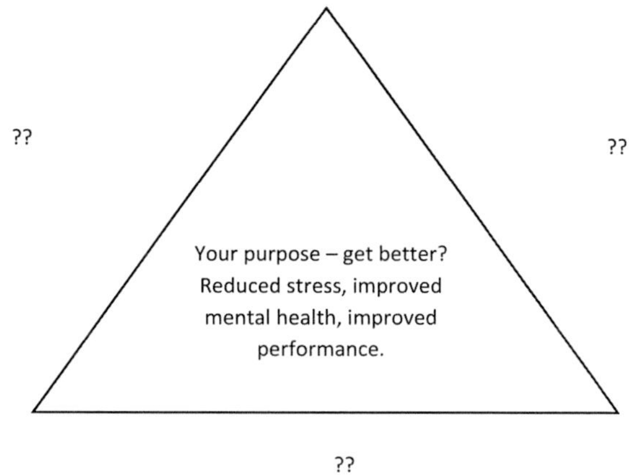

Action: Purpose (I aim to get better) is not enough. To get better it helps to identify what drives you on – why should you get better?

"Hero of the past: Edith Cavell – Patriotism is not enough".

32. Get your sleep.

    Sleep is important. I believe that I can handle pretty much anything if I can get my sleep. Sleep is a very interesting topic. Sleep is one of the classic things that is disturbed when you are at high stress levels and under mental health attack. We all need different amounts of it, and the amount we need varies by age. Research shows that regular sleep is more important than the exact amount. Sleep can also vary in quality as well as quantity, as we move through the 5 stages and depths of sleep. It has helped me to be aware of what I call my 4 "grades" of sleep.

Grade A – how much I ideally need to function at an optimum way.

For me this is 8 hrs per night – the figure for the average person is 7hrs 40 mins. If I get this every day I can operate at 95%+ efficiency levels every day.

Grade B – how much I need to function at 80% of my capability. This is where I can do the job quite well, but I am not at my creative or sparkly best.

For me this is 6 hours.

Grade C - how much I need to function at all.

For me its 4 hours – if I get this I can get through the day. I will not be good but I can function. The worst feeling is usually before breakfast, once you are into the day, you should be OK.

Grade D – unable to function – take the day off or rest immediately or the sleep problem will escalate fast.

For me this is less than 4 hours.

What are your sleep grades? How many hours do you need per night?

Grade	Operating capability	Hours per night for you?
A	Ideal / Optimal	
B	Satisfactory but not ideal – can do most things well but not buzzing/sparkling or 100% creative.	
C	Can function – working from reserves.	
D	Cannot function	

You might consider keeping a sleep log for a few nights to see if that helps. I use these metrics to encourage me if I have had a bad night. So even if I get 4 hours I'm in the game. But I recognise that I cannot only get 4 hours every night. Most of us also need some "wind down time". Like a mechanical fan, it takes time after we switch off the power for the blade to stop turning. Finishing work at a set time each day, and then watching TV is a good switch off technique. A problem which is now growing for younger leaders is that they use their phone as an alarm clock and take emails on their phones, something I have resisted. So, when they go to their bedroom they can still receive incoming texts, snapchats and email messages. "Incoming" fires the nervous system and stimulates the secretion of adrenaline and other hormones, designed to keep you alert and awake.

Here are my top tips for sleep:

- Know your 4 grades of sleep – use this to help you. You can run off grade B (and even grade C) for a short period.
- Regularity of sleep is even more important than how much you get.
- Early nights work, but you can't "catch up" sleep on a one-for-one hourly basis.
- If you or your partner are experiencing a problem with sleep – don't sleep together! (But don't sleep with someone else either, unless you want to create another 'All Black' to add to the list!).
- One of the biggest factors in getting to sleep is warmth. Get yourself warm and snuggle down.
- A good mattress, a good pillow a comfortable bed with good ventilation help.
- Keep a notepad by your bed and if you really have things on your mind dump them in the notepad if you wake up at night.
- Don't worry if you can't get to sleep immediately. You can relax the mind and body if you are awake so you might actually be getting more rest than you think.
- Sleep is the end activity of a shutdown programme, which can be accelerated though proactive routines and conditioning. If you do the same thing each night in the same order you can condition the body to shut off faster.

- Turn off all 'incoming' (phones, I-pads, laptops) one hour before sleep and leave them in a separate room.

Further reading: Why we sleep. Matthew Walker. 2017.

Action: Understand how much sleep you need, the impact it has on your operating capability, and work on routines to make sure you get enough.

33. Use catnaps to 'power up'.

One of the skills I leant as a young man from the military was the skill to catnap. This is to go to sleep fast for 10-20 minutes and then wake up. A useful skill if you are on 'stag' sentry duty during the night. Also, a regular bus journey to school as a teenager meant that I was able to use the noise and movement of the bus as trigger for a quick nap. It's amazing how just a few minutes can revitalise you. If I have had a particularly bad night (level B or C), I will now go to bed for 20 mins in the mid-afternoon and power-up. I accept that this is easier if you work for yourself and control your hours, only the most enlightened boss will welcome you asleep at your desk mid-afternoon! Like many skills, the more you practise, the better you are at it. I suggest you practise it when you are not stressed so you can utilise it when you need it. It's a bit like learning a martial art, don't wait until you are in the fight or competition, before you need it, build up the skill so it's ready. Again this skill can be honed using 'Pavlovian response' techniques where stimuli can be used to trigger a fast dive into sleep e.g. music, food, going upstairs etc. It also gives you a great feeling of control.

Action: Use catnaps to 'power up': 10-20 mins will boost you.

34. Beware of the pre-dawn raid.

My friend who is ex-special forces tells me that a good time to attack is just before dawn. There are many reasons for this. One is to do with sleep patterns. Most of us fall off to sleep say at 22.00/23.00 ish and then pass through light sleep, stage one, into deeper sleep levels and then into REM sleep (Rapid Eye Movement), which is where dreaming takes place. As we move into sustained deeper sleep, the body itself turns down all dials and lowers defences and relaxes. The trough of this curve for most of us is about 03.00/04.00. We are at our most vulnerable then, so a good time for enemy special forces to raid us. It is normal for us to toss and turn many times during the night and wake-up many times. So don't panic if you do this. Sometimes this can be linked to food and drink. A large meal before bedtime, certain foods, and alcohol, make sleep harder. Knowing your personal 'sleep-raiding foods' and drinks can help. Cocoa (or stiff drink) can help some to sleep, while it might keep others awake. It is also normal for us to perspire when dreaming. So, don't panic if you do this. It is also normal from about 04.00/05.00 for the body to start to wake up from our deepest sleep and at this point the subconscious mind opens the door to the conscious and often floods it with all the things it has been working on in the night. Many people wake up fast at this time and can't get back to sleep. Understanding that this is all normal and natural, helps. You have just overloaded your brain with things to think about and it is trying to help. It is your mind's attempt to solve the problems you asked it to when you went to bed. Have your pen and paper by your bed. Capture all the answers your subconscious has given you. If the pre-dawn raid comes, expect it, deal with it, and then roll over back to sleep, or at least rest, and slow down the firestorm of ideas. When you rise, congratulate yourself for having successfully dealt with the raid, or if no raid came, be pleased that you got a complete night's sleep.

Action: Expect the pre-dawn raid, deal with it, roll over.

35. Identify your "stay awake issue".

I learnt this one from my good friend and fellow board member Tim Sutton. We all have things that we carry around with us that we worry about and work on. One of his techniques as a Non-Executive Director, was to ask the exec, and the rest of the non-execs, what their top concern was, i.e. what is your "stay awake issue". So-called as this is the thing most likely to cause a raid on your sleep. In military circles these have been called a "fizzer" or a "fast burner", from bomb fuses. We would then see what we could all do as a board to help the individual with theirs. Interestingly sometimes your stay awake issue will be the same as others, and at other times, yours will be unique. Most of us spend more time worrying about our stay awake issue than we do sharing it or working on solutions. We found that sharing and discussing our stay awake issues at board meetings helped us all.

Action: Identify your "stay awake issue" – and share it.

36. Turn off the kit.

    Incoming messages from our phones can be a source of stress or if not stressful, keep our engines running in the problem-solving mode, and restrict our rest and recovery opportunities. Chemicals are realised into our body when we receive incoming communications. This problem has grown in recent years as work has moved from 'somewhere we go' to 'something we do'. We have been given the power, something that previous generations have not had, the power to choose when we do it. Just like in the 'all you can eat buffet', just because it is there, it does not mean it is a good thing to continue eating, until you are sick. There are various solutions to this all-invasive tech attack, like having a work and a private phone, or not having your emails on your phone. The most practical action is simply to 'turn off all incoming' between certain hours, and if it helps, tell your colleagues you are doing this. It might also help their stress levels too. Very few things can't wait until tomorrow. Our bodies and minds do need time to shut down, recover and restore, so we can go again.

    Action: Turn off the kit – between certain hours – let your phone sleep!

37. Go for 'walk and talk', and don't talk about "it".

    Sometimes we need a space NOT to talk about our stay awake issue. Sometimes it is useful to be able to get all the benefits of walking, and not think about the main issue. A good technique here is to fill your mind with other things to talk about. The deeper the conversation on the other issues, no matter how trivial, the better. If one major issue is dominating our lives then having a normal conversation about the ordinary or mundane, or about people and relationships outside the situation, or about great things to look forward to in the future, is more helpful than talking about the big issue.

    Action: Go for 'walk and talk', and don't talk about 'it'.

38. Take the 'monkey' off your back.

    It is much harder to operate if you have a 'monkey' crawling all over your back. A monkey is not major stressor ('All Black') but is an irritant, distracter, energy sapper or time waster. It might be something you have accepted for yourself, or one your colleagues have given to you. It could be a voluntary activity or something you have agreed to do when you really do not have the time. We all say yes to stuff that is not critical and then end up being distracted by it. This can be Ok when you are operating normally but you cannot afford to have things crawling all over you when you are focussed on doing the big stuff. Take the monkey off your back but try not to give it to one of your colleagues!

    Further reading: Get That Monkey Off Your Back: Helpful hints guide to a happier and healthy lifestyle. Helpful guide to stress and self-esteem. Debra Fleming. 2005.

    Action: Take the "monkey" off your back, and don't accept monkeys.

39. Don't give power away to difficult people.

    In our working and personal lives, we all know people who suck energy and are difficult. Often, we end up investing disproportionate amounts of energy into these people who might not be adding value to the job in hand. We need a way of dealing with this. If we know this and do nothing, anxiety builds up and it can get to an extreme situation when even a missed call or an email from this person causes an extreme stress response in us. The key thing is to identify your difficult people and decide how you will handle them. Review how much power you are giving them and whether throttling back of this might help? Alternatively, you might consider how and when you engage with them: some people are less difficult face-to-face than they are with email or phone. Taking the initiative in this way, and initiating the contact, usually helps rather than waiting for them to engage.

    Action: Don't give power away to difficult people – take the initiative, decide in advance how you will engage with them.

40. Don't try to enlighten the "unconscious".

Another sort of person to keep an eye open for are the "unconscious". Their minds are full and no matter how much energy you invest in them, they will not agree with you or even understand what you are saying. They have decided their view on you or your project prior to the engagement. There is an old fable where the western journalist goes to meet the Tibetan Monk to learn about Buddhism. On arriving at the temple at the top of the hill the journalist is warmly greeted by the monk. "Can you tell me all there is to know about Buddhism?" says the journalist. "First we have tea" says the monk. He pours the tea into a cup and fills it, and then keeps pouring until it overflows. He then says ... "The lesson is over" ... and leaves. The point being the journalist could never learn anything about Buddhism as his cup (mind) was already full! He was unconscious. I have spent far too much of my time as a leader trying to enlighten the unconscious. Their cups were full. They were never going to get it, agree to it, or follow me. I would have been better advised to have invested my energies in other ways. With mental health, be sensitive to people who are trying to help you, whose cups are full. Sometimes we need to look ourselves in the mirror and see if our own cups are full too! If your cup is full with the belief you cannot get better, then you will not get better. Challenge yourself and others if you detect a cup-full situation.

"Don't make journeys to enlighten the unconscious".

Action: Don't try to enlighten the "unconscious" – their cups are full.

41. A change is better than a rest.

    When we are busy, we all crave to do 'nothing'. But doing nothing can be hard, and unless the brain is engaged, it can be a time when worry escalates but you are not on the front line to be able to move the problems forward. For many leaders, this might be when you are taking time off with the family. For many entrepreneurs and the self-employed, it is when they are not working that things often appear the most stressful, as business never stops. A good way of dealing with this is to fill your 'down' time with a displacement activity, something that requires your focus but is different to the day job. This could be music, or playing sport, or watching sport, or playing with the children, doing your hobby such as beekeeping etc. Often when stress levels build we tend to cut down on these restorative activities. Interestingly the greater the physical, emotional, mental, spiritual, and financial commitment the greater and therefore more valuable the displacement activity can be.

    Action: An engaged change is better than a rest. Step up your displacement activity.

42. The Art of Action.

    With bookstores and bookshelves jammed with leadership and management books, it can still be hard to find a good one that adds practical insight to help the modern leader. But the "The Art of Action" by Stephen Bungay is just one of those, and worth a read. Stephen is an Englishman who has specialised in Anglo German history. Stephen uses his love of history to delve into the practices and culture of the 19th century Prussian Army, and the thinking of Generals Clausewitz and Von Moltke, exploring a leadership and management system, that was so profound, it has formed the bedrock of the most successful military academies and military leadership philosophies around the world for the last 200 years.

    Further reading: The Art of Action: How Leaders Close the Gaps between Plans, Actions and Results. Stephen Bungay. 2010.

The book contrasts the efficient and effective leadership approach of the Prussian military with what happens in business today, and in doing so, provokes the reader to reflect on what is going on in their own businesses. Reading books is always a personal journey but here are 3 things that I picked up from the book:

1. Most people in most modern organisations do not understand what the strategy is and what it means for them. Be clear on what really matters (strategic intent). Tell managers what you are doing and why (and keep it simple). Provide managers with space and support them, and ask them "how they are going to do it". Apply this to mental health – what is your intent and how does that link to your recovery plan?
2. There are always big gaps between plans, actions and results. "No plan survives first contact with the enemy". This is the natural state of things, mainly driven by the concept of FRICTION, as soon as the plan is deployed things start going off plan – due to things going wrong, misinterpretations, complications, unforeseen obstacles, accidents, weather, sickness, competitor moves etc. The leader's job is to close these gaps. Apply this to mental health – expect things not to go to plan, and for the need to continually adjust.
3. The nature of most things is that they cannot be controlled from the centre. Attempts to do so actually make the situation worse. Bungay argues for "Independent thinking obedience" where managers close to the action have the power to respond to the unfolding local situation. This is also known as "directed opportunism". Do not command more than is necessary. Do not plan beyond what you can foresee. The best leaders use their experience to recognise patterns in the unfolding situation based on their experience and instinct to make quick and effective decisions close to the action. They can only do this if they understand the overall strategic intent of their superiors. Apply this to mental health – be clear on your overall intent; do not think about your health more than is necessary; do

not plan for recovery greater than you can foresee; choose action based on your unfolding health situation.

Action: "Art of Action" – be clear about your intent and link this to a clear response plan; expect things not to go to plan, make decisions close to the action given the unfolding situation.

43. Do not empower others with an expectation that they have the answer – you might be disappointed.

We explored when we looked at myths that there might not be AN answer. But we might go around empowering others with an expectation that they can supply us with it. When you are in the formal health care system there is a danger that you become the passive recipient of expert advice and direction. There is also a danger that you will be looking for an answer, a silver bullet to your situation. Experience shows that often conditions have multiple and inter-related causes and symptoms. So, there might not be AN answer. Some turn to alternative experts outside the formal health care system to see if they have THE answer. There might be many answers or none. It can be disappointing to empower the experts with an expectation that they can find the answer, and when this does not materialise, you slide further down the health curve. Experts can help, and they can be part of you moving toward better health, but they might not be able to give you the answer you are looking for.

Action: Accept that you should not empower others with an expectation that they have the answer – you might be disappointed.

44. Have a "Cobra" meeting.

When there is a national crisis the Prime Minister can call for a meeting of the Cobra Committee. Cobra stands for Cabinet Office Briefing Room A, named after where it was first purported to meet. From this room, senior politicians and security experts receive intelligence and make decisions to manage a response to the unfolding crisis. This has several benefits. It brings decision makers together with the latest information and it gives a signal to others that something is being done, which can raise morale. One mental health management technique is to give yourself a 'Cobra' meeting at regular intervals, daily, weekly etc., to review the current position and progress. It helps in that it releases you so you are not talking about the progress, or lack of it, continually, but the items can be parked for the cobra meeting agenda. The meeting might be with a team of your own experts or supporters, as with the Prime Minister, or it might be on your own as a "daily solo" where you allocate some thinking and review space in the day.

Action: Have a "cobra" meeting – with others or a daily/ weekly solo, to review current position, review progress and raise morale.

45. Control, and Influence, and Canute.

One of the most effective tools that I have used with leaders to quickly deal with stress is the concept of 'circles of control and influence'. We all face 3 types of problems – those we can control, those we cannot control but can influence, and those we can neither control nor influence.

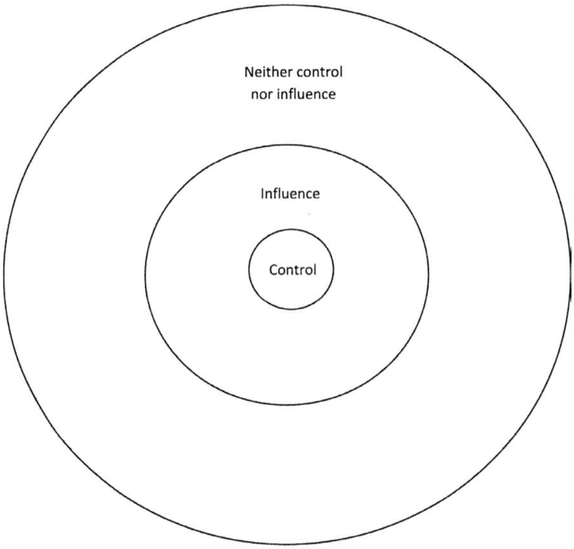

How would you plot in your current top 10 challenges? Which circle do they fall within?

If you ask people to draw the diagram with areas representing relative impact, this is how most people draw the diagram:

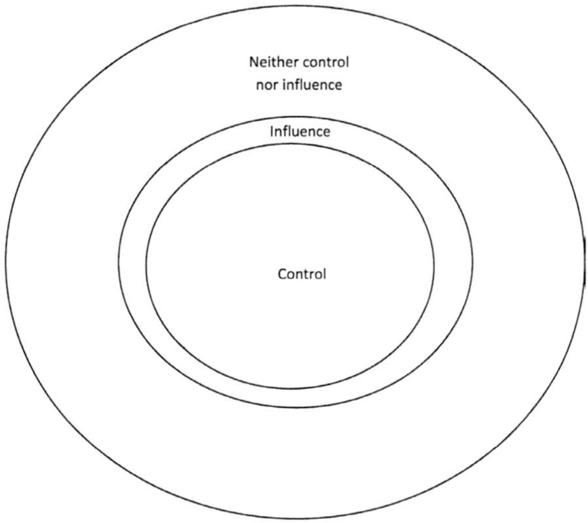

This means that most people, particularly leaders, think they have a lot of control, their influence is only a bit and there is a lot which is outside their control and influence. Research has shown that in reality, this is how it usually looks:

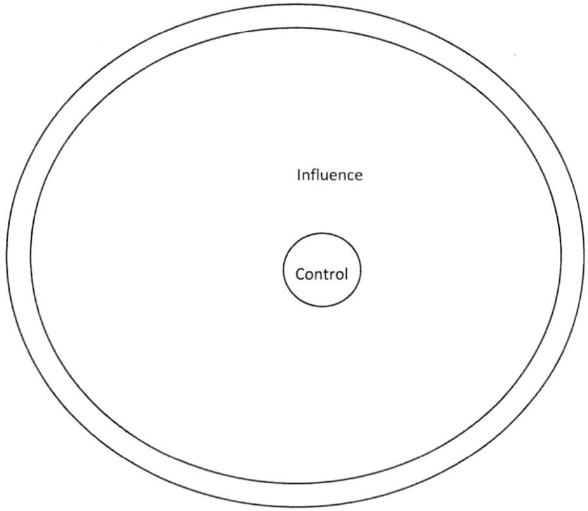

The implications being: we can control a lot less than we think. But we have much more influence than we think! Accepting what we can control (very little) and what we can influence (quite a lot) very much helps when considering our mental health. One of the main drivers of poor mental health is the feeling that we are out of control - our poor health (illness) is controlling us. If you start to feel this, challenge yourself and ask what can you influence, you will be surprised that this list can get quite long. It should raise your morale.

King Canute The Great, was the first Viking King to successfully rule over the truly united realm of England (and Denmark, Norway and parts of Sweden), from the year 1016. This religious-minded Viking warrior won acclaim for his respect for the old English laws, and ruled with a keen sense of justice. Many of us have been brought up with the idea that Canute was a stupid King, intoxicated with power and his iconic moment is when Canute famously had his throne carried to the seashore and then, sitting on it, commanded the waves to advance no further. But there is another explanation of his actions, which is far more interesting. His flattering courtiers claimed that he was "So great, he could command the tides of the sea to go back". When the tides did the inevitable, and refused to obey him, he is said to have cleverly demonstrated that although the deeds of kings appeared "great" in the minds of men, they were as nothing in the face of God's power.

Canute's inspiration is to teach us that often no one individual, no matter how charismatic, powerful or famous, has complete control. He also reminds us that our businesses operate within an environment, much of which we cannot control. A rising tide lifts all the boats at sea, while a falling tide strands many on the beach. We might not be able to command the tides, but we can position our businesses to take advantage, or be at risk from, external events. If we stand still, eventually we will be either left high and dry on the beach, or swept away to sea! With our mental health consider what you can control, what you can influence and what you can neither control nor influence.

Action: Control or influence - accept that you can control little, but influence a lot. Be a wise King Canute.

"Hero of the past - King Canute".

46. Cut the "salami".

    When we are highly stressed we tend to see the whole problem as one. "Cutting the salami" is to cut the whole into it bite-sized chunks. It's the answer to 'How do you eat an elephant?' The answer, one small piece at a time. Most problems are easier to move forward if you are focused on dealing with or solving one element at a time. You can then digest the pieces in a sensible in order.

    Action: Cut the "salami" – view the whole as a series of digestible chunks.

47. Play one touch.

    I started my working career in days before the I-Phone, before internet, and before email. Communications were via a thing called letters, and these were typed by secretaries in the typing pool. One of the best tools I ever learnt was the one touch rule – touch a piece of paper only once. My boss used to say keep your in-tray empty and touch it once. This rule applies as much to emails and digital comms as it does to the tactile world. Opening something up, looking at it and putting it aside to deal with, or worse pick up and put down again, not only wastes time, but can set the subconscious into streams of worry. Modern media and IT is very good at rapidly increasing the speed at which we are required to deal with things. Of course, there are exceptions, where 'sleeping on it' or putting it aside to reflect on can help but most communications can be dealt with, with one touch. Open – action now.

My 'default behaviours' for all incoming emails are: DELETE (best option – no action required); or REPLY NOW (if I can do fast); or PRINT TO ACTION LATER (in which case when you return to it, touch it only once). This keeps my email box permanently empty. I work through the printed emails later, when I have the time or when serious drafting is needed. We are all different and different approaches will be suitable for each of us, but you can start by noticing how many times you "touch" each piece of communication. If you are in the habit of touching them more than once, bring in a one-touch rule and see your efficiency soar.

Action: Play "one touch" – deal with a piece of communications only once.

48. Deploy 'relaxation techniques'.

    There are many techniques that can help you relax. For example: mindfulness, hypnosis, Pilates, yoga, meditation, reflexology, dance. I must admit, I have tried most of these, and most are not up my street. I prefer competitive sports as a relaxation technique, but I accept that these are also not for everyone. The message is to try these techniques and find ones you enjoy. If you enjoy them you will be prepared to apply yourself to them. My mother-in-law Barbara has always been against going to the gym, but would happily spend the morning cleaning her house and her afternoon doing gardening: stretching, reaching, lifting, bending, twisting, and crouching. When her grandchildren boasted they that had done one hour in the gym – she would say she had done 6 hours' exercise at home, 3 inside cleaning and 3 outside in the garden!

    Action: Deploy relaxation techniques. Try them and adopt the ones you enjoy.

49. Understand the "mental laws".

    The study of psychology and psychotherapy has identified that there are certain "mental laws". Experts argue that our brain operates in accordance with these laws, pretty much like the natural world operates under the laws of nature (gravity, tides etc). Like the natural laws, they operate 100% of the time, whether you believe in them or not. Understanding how your brain operates and what the mental laws are, can help if you are a conceptual or intellectual thinker. The laws include control, belief, cause and effect, expectation, correspondence, attitude, and substitution. Hundreds of books have been written on this. I will try to offer summaries in a paragraph:

Law of Control - you cannot solve a problem you cannot control, but we control very little. Focus on the aspects of your stress and health that you can control.

Law of Belief – what you believe is true. If you believe you will get better, you are right. If you believe you will not get better, you are right. Changing your belief changes your truth. Believe you will get better and that you are getting better.

Law of Cause and Effect – for every effect there is a cause. Ill health is an effect; find the cause. Health is an effect; find the cause.

Law of Expectation – you get, not what you want, but what you expect. Expect to get better.

Law of Correspondence - you will be attracted to situations and people consistent with your place in the world. Surround yourself with healthy people who talk and act healthily. Ditch negative and ill people who talk about illness.

Law of Attitude - attitude can be changed instantly and it is the greatest single factor in determining outcomes. Change your attitude about your stress and health, and your outcomes will improve.

Law of Substitution - your brain can only hold one thought at a time. You decide if it is positive or negative. Substitute negative with positive thoughts.

If you can relate to these laws, it might be helpful to construct an action plan based on them.

Mental laws action plan:

		Action for you:
Law of Control	Focus on what you can control.	
Law of Belief	Adopt positive beliefs about your health and recovery. Believe you will and are, getting better.	
Law of Cause and Effect	Understand the cause of your ill health, and health.	
Law of Expectation	Expect to get better.	
Law of Correspondence	Surround yourself with healthy people.	
Law of Attitude	Adopt a positive attitude about your health.	
Law of Substitution	Substitute negative thoughts with positive ones.	

Action: If you are a thinker - understand and live life consistent with the "mental laws".

50. De-personalise.

Most leaders over-personalise things. Personalising is a strong leadership trait and regarded as a key magnetic feature of strong leadership for many followers. However when it comes to mental health, over-personalising the situation may be harmful. Treat the condition or your health as though it is something outside you, as a business problem or operational challenge to solve, and you might immediately start to feel better. Sometimes it is good to over-personalise the solution and action but it is usually more helpful to de-personalise the problem and situation.

Action: De-personalise your situation.

51. Play the game your way.

When I was at Wimbledon this year (watching not playing), I came across a statue and this story. After winning in straight sets the Wimbledon gentlemen's singles in 1934, Fred Perry was in the changing room bathing. Custom was, for a committee member to present the tie and champagne to the champion. Perry found his tie left over the back of a chair and the champagne was given to the runner up, and Perry overheard them saying to his opponent "Congratulations, this was one day when the best man didn't win!" This working-class lad from the North, who learnt to play on public courts next to a housing estate, never felt accepted by the upper-class elite. He was furious. Later it is claimed, he was turned away from the club for not wearing his tie!

Perry's achievements:

- The greatest player in the history of British tennis.
- Three consecutive men's Wimbledon singles championships 1934-36, while he was world number one.
- Ten majors (8 grand slams and 2 pro slams) and six doubles, (including Wimbledon mixed) and the first man ever to win all four Grand Slams, aged 26.
- Helping Britain dominate the Davis Cup - 4 consecutive victories 1934-36. Perry won 34 of his 38 rubbers (11 out of 14 doubles).
- His 1936 Wimbledon final win of: 6-1, 6-1, 6-0, lasted less than 45 mins, the fastest final of the 20th century.
- Record holder of 55 consecutive set wins in the US open and 62 at Wimbledon.
- World table tennis champion aged 19.
- Kick-started the professional tennis era, exemplifying fitness, determination and ruthlessness to win, combined with celebrity good looks and a slick dress sense.
- And went on to make money from a retail brand selling "Fred Perry" (laurel logo) clothing, ironic for a story that started with a tie.

This lad from Stockport, whose father was a cotton spinner, trade unionist and was in the Cooperative Labour Party; had a tense relationship with authority, especially with Wimbledon, or more correctly the All England Lawn Tennis and Croquet Club. A relationship only fully reconciled when his statue was erected in 1984. Interestingly, within the snobbery, prejudiced class prism and values of the 1930s:

- He was seen to be rude and discourteous to opponents and umpires, including not congratulating fellows for a good shot or apologising for luck, and using sarcastic language such as "very clevah" if he was beaten by a shot.
- This "upstart" took winning far too seriously, was far too outspoken, and did not exhibit the gentlemanly qualities expected.
- He embraced too easily professionalism and "money making" and was banned as a professional from playing on LTA courts, his membership rescinded and the tie was taken back!
- He would glare at umpires ... and even worse, he would use his trademark leap over the net when he had won, a most unseemly act.

We can now see, looking back, that his story captures the clash of the "Amateur Gentlemen" vs. the "Performance Professional". The former were the mainly public school boy custodians of the spirit of the game, of tradition, ethos, values, sportsmanship and behaviours. The latter, provide a laser focus and obsession on performance, continuous improvement, learning and winning. How appropriate that England's best ever tennis player captures the essence of our nation's journey through sport; and how appropriate that the bronze statue of the sport's highest performer is placed in the rose garden outside the member's enclosure of one of our oldest clubs. On that day in 1984 Perry said that the placing of the statue meant more to him than "all the prize money in the world".

Your health is your game – you should play it as you see fit. Try to blend the best of the amateur - keep your spirits high, attitude right and be values-led. But from the professional, look for continuous improvement, learn, be obsessed with getting better, and expect to fully recover. Take advice from your coaches, officials, friends and family but if you are to have great health, you need to play the game yourself, your way.

"Hero of the past: Fred Perry –
who played the game his way."

Action: Blend the best of the amateur and professional, and play your health game your way – be true to yourself.

52. Step up your sport / exercise regime.

    The important words here are 'step up' and 'regime'. If you exercise 4 times a week – go to 5. By stepping up your exercising you will be raising your ability to deal with the stress as the stress levels rise. You are actively responding to the negative with a positive to cancel it out. If you are like me, and already do a lot of sport, go from 5 sessions to 6. If you don't do any, do not try 6 sessions a week; you will not sustain it. Thirty minutes per session is enough for body and mind, you do not need to run a marathon or book a double session of squash! Also get yourself a regime, a routine. Try to do the exercise at set times in the week, regardless of how the day has been or your stress levels are at that moment. This will enable you to stabilise your response energy levels and emotions, to high stress. It is also worth noting that we each have circadian rhythm. I am good for work in the morning and evening. I dip late afternoon, so this is when I exercise to boost myself. Certain sports are good for certain types of recovery. Ball chasing / explosive sports are good for a complete switch off (hockey, football, squash, tennis). I do not worry about work when I am chasing around the court or pitch after that ball. You are never too old. In my fifties and after a 30-year break, I took up competitive 5-a-side football again this year, playing with my gifted younger brother Paul. This is something I never thought I would do: brilliant! Other sports are good to allow your brain to order things, problem solve or come up with ideas (cycling, walking, running). I used to have an office next to the health club in our village and at 15.00hrs most days I would go for a swim. My staff would comment that after I had had my swim, I would come back not only refreshed but with loads of new ideas and their workload would rise exponentially! Again, do the things you enjoy. If you need the encouragement or discipline of another person, get yourself a personal trainer, or training buddy. Most of us cut sport/exercise down when stress and mental health attack hits; we need to step it up.

Action: Step up sport / exercise regime.

"With my son, Jake in a rare appearance in a team together in Hockey – Jake's much better than me".

53. Obsess about being a mental athlete, not a mental patient.

A patient is "*a person receiving or registered to receive medical treatment*". 'Receiving' is a passive activity. If you view yourself as a patient you have given over responsibility and control of your own health to someone else. Patients are associated with illness and not wellness. A better way, is to view yourself as a mental athlete, albeit someone who is not currently performing. An athlete is "*a person who is proficient in sports and other forms of physical exercise*". For me, viewing myself as athlete and not a patient, helped me. Note the emphasis here is on **proficient** (good, active, progressive) as opposed to **recipient** (bad, passive, preventing deterioration). If an athlete is not performing, they gather around them their support team (medical doctor, psychologist, nutritionist, strength and conditioning coach, tacticians). They expect to perform well in the future. They know that by applying many different approaches they will be able to improve their performance step by step, back to what it was or higher. They have the mindset of a winner. If you are obsessive or a worrier, as many champions are, channel this obsession into improved athletic performance.

Action: Obsess about being a mental athlete, not a mental patient.

54. Borrow models / paradigms from things that interest you.

As you might have gathered, I have an interest in history and sport! I have been able to manage my own health by constructing the health problem and seeing it within the world or paradigm of history or sport. The paradigm you prefer is not important. It might be Formula 1, or Harry Potter or Western Films or TV Comedy Programmes or Physics. The point is, for most of us the world of medicine can be a foreign land clouded in foreign culture and a foreign language. Turning the situation into something that you know something about or have some interest in, is both comforting and can be fun. It also engages you intellectually and creatively, and enables you to reach new insights, as well as raising morale. This is all good for mental health. Getting the problem into a language and paradigm that you are comfortable with, rather than the language of medical professionals and the language of illness, can improve both your understanding of the problem and your disposition to act. If you are an engineer, think "how can I fix, or put together my mental health". If a sportsman, "how do I get a podium finish?".

Action: Borrow models / paradigms from things that interest you, and construct your health problem within the framework of a world that interests you.

55. Use routines to help turn yourself on and off.

    The natural rhythm of life is that your body and mind like to have periods of work followed by periods of rest. On, then off. One of the great challenges of leaders in the internet age is that our external environment often makes it hard for us to turn off. So, we all need to work smarter to make sure we can turn off. Routines are the easiest way to do this. Do the same thing, the same way, at the same time, and your body gets conditioned to warming up or warming down with the triggers. If you want a good night's sleep have the same set of steps you go through each night at the same time: this will help you switch off. If your work is mainly desk based, having routines which block work into types such as analysis, emails, creative, responding, reflection, etc can also help. Many small business owners, particularly in the sectors of digital and marketing, are structuring the day for their staff into "email / working alone" time vs. "chatting, coffee and collaborative" time. If you can set up daily routines for different types of working, this can help. The more you practise the routines, the more efficient the process will become.

    Action: Use routines to help turn yourself on and off.

56. Hobbies OTBC.

    Hobbies are good, in that you can lose yourself in them, focusing on something that is completely removed from the issues you have upper-most in your mind. Supporting a football team and making the pilgrimage to the ground every fortnight to the home games is good therapy, as my mum Pam, and mother in law Barbara, will testify. They are fans of Norwich City FC (whose signature tune is one of the oldest football songs in the world "On the Ball City" – OTBC). Not only are you on the move (which is good) but you become part of something bigger (the crowd), and for a brief moment, reality is suspended as you become a fan (short for 'fanatic' ... someone filled with excessive zeal and delusion about a cause!). The exercise, the distraction, being part of something bigger than yourself is all good for mental health. Even the post-match whinge or phone in programme (Canary Call) can be part of this therapy.

Action: Hobbies - On the Ball City – step up, take up, or revisit an enjoyable hobby that gets you on the move and enables you to immerse yourself for a short while in another world.

57. Do today's business today and leave tomorrow's for another day.

    Most of us try to fit too much in each day. We over-commit. We don't allow ourselves slack or room to manoeuvre. We end up running late. We work long hours. We tire ourselves out. We cut out the time and space for us to manoeuvre, reflect and respond, when things change, as they always do. The old enemy "being busy" gets in the way of agility, creativity and effectiveness. In most businesses, people are busier than they have ever been. Some things do need doing today. Remember Churchill's favourite sticker he placed on his papers in WW2 was "Action this day". But a lot of what we do today can wait until tomorrow (or next week). It is often ourselves who put pressure on us, by expecting us to do it today. Of course, emails and texts speed up and pile on more pressure to respond instantly to everything. If you are not careful you can charge around like a headless chicken responding to everything that comes in. One test is how often you check your emails or phone. Most people do this over 10 times a day, some do it hundreds of times per day. Back in the 1970s we used to open the post once a day! Do you need to check emails or your phone as often as you do? I am not convinced things are more efficient now. In fact, even though we are moving faster some things seem to take longer. Dealing with more and more incoming communications means you can spend your time catching and sorting stuff and not actually actioning it. But, if you have started something try to finish it. General Wellington put a lot of his success down to finishing a day's business in one day. Completing something raises morale and allows you to switch off better and rest.

Action: Does it need doing today? If so 'Action this Day' (Churchill) and 'Complete this Day' (Wellington). Otherwise leave until tomorrow.

58. What's coming over the fence? Cricket balls, pineapples, cuddly toys, paper weights, hand grenades and unexploded bombs.

At the height of my recent stress it felt like standing on one side of the garden fence and having to deal with objects coming over in random order, and fast, and in varying bursts of intensity. Sometimes nothing would come over and then you would get a burst of objects. The fence in this case was my PC. I classified the things I had to deal with as follows: cricket balls, pineapples, cuddly toys, paper weights, hand grenades and unexploded bombs.

Dealing with some of these items well, was critical, others were less important. You must decide how you are going to handle each issue and when. What is the nature of the issue? Do you need to deal with it at all, and if so, does it need dealing with now?

Here is how you deal with them:

Cricket balls – this is what we need for later. They need to be sorted by colour. Catch them and neatly store them for later use. You can sort them as they come in if you have time, or later.

Pineapples – these are for eating, but they need to be cut up. Put them in a separate pile and cut them up later, not now, as this is time-consuming.

Cuddly toys – cute but useless, keep, but give away later.

Paper weights – useless, throw in the bin immediately.

Hand grenades – throw back immediately. Failing to deal with them fast, will cause a major problem. They need to be on the other side of the fence to you.

Unexploded bomb – careful. Place down for diffusing later. They need to be dealt with soon but not immediately.

If the incoming rate is fast, it can be very tiring just standing still. Top tip: control your time at the fence, turn off communications. Have a communications-free window.

Action: If you are spending too much time at the 'fence', don't. Turn off your communications. When you are there, classify items as they come in. Decide which you will deal with now, and which later.

59. Intimacy with your partner

    I am not going to say too much here as my children will read this manual. But when one or both in a partnership are under extreme stress or mental health attack, intimacy in its many forms, tends to get squeezed out as we become "too tired". This can be in the obvious form of making love, but also in terms of cuddling, touching, listening, smiling, being in the moment, asking how they are, and caring for your partner's needs. It is possible to find one of the pair caring for the needs of others at work and at home, and the main partner coming last in the queue behind children, parents, friends, and work. When it is their turn, the energy tank is empty. Intimacy improves the mental health of you and your partner, regardless of who initiates it. I once asked two very successful individuals, married for 50 years, what was the secret of their relationship, they said "10 mins". They spent 10 minutes a day in each other's company looking after and taking care of the other.

    Action: Make time (10 mins) to be intimate with your partner and care for them each day.

60. Use Project Management Methodology.

    If you are an experienced manager you will be familiar with Project Management Methodology (PMM). PMM has been used in many organisations as an alternative to 'Business as Usual'. PMM is where activities are viewed as discreet projects or programmes that cut across the organisation in terms of the traditional structure. Projects have four identifying features:

    Time

    Cost / resource

    Scope

    Risk

    Management of these variables is crucial to the successful delivery of the project. They are usually set out in detail in the form of a 'project plan'. If we view getting better as a project – can you prepare a plan under these 4 headings for your recovery?

PMM Variable	Health plan? Action to take.	Monitored by?
Time		
Cost / resource		
Scope		
Risk		

Action: Use Project Management Methodology – use time, cost/resource, scope and risk to plan for a great recovery.

61. Hero of the past – General Slim. Don't underestimate having a good plan.

General, later Field Marshall, William (Bill) Slim was the commander of "Forgotten" 14th Army in Burma. Slim is regarded by many experts as the best general of WW2 and by some as "the greatest military Commander of the 20th Century".

Following one of the worst and most humiliating military defeats in British history, the fall of Singapore, the British were pushed back, suffering a 900-mile retreat through Burma. The 14th Army was composed of a poorly equipped mix of empire troops, of Indian (Hindu, Sikh and Muslim), British, African, and others: many languages, many cultures. They were at the end of a long logistical pipeline, and facing appalling terrain, weather, disease, and a ferocious enemy. But despite all this, by the strength of his leadership, Slim turned them around into an efficient fighting unit with incredible spirit which would go on to defeat the 'invincible' Japanese army.

In his book 'Defeat into Victory' Slim sets out many useful tips for the leader. He was loved by his men and affectionately known as "Uncle Bill". Max Hastings: "His calm, robust style of leadership and concern for the interests of his men won the admiration of all who served under him ... His blunt honesty, lack of bombast and unwillingness to play courtier did him few favours in the corridors of power. Only his soldiers never wavered in their devotion".

Fighting in the jungle is pretty stressful, and reading Slim, I have lifted out three top tips that I found useful in my own journey from Defeat to Victory...

Beware of the bad idea fairy. When dealing with your own mental health you will be presented with lots of ideas and advice from health professionals, family and friends. Many of these ideas will not be good! Some will be harmful! Slim: "... persuasive young men interested in selling short cuts to victory…these 'racketeers', as I called them, were of two kinds, those whose acquaintance with war was confined to large non-fighting staffs where they had time to develop their theories; and tough, cheerful fellows who might be first-class landed on a beach at night to scupper a sentry-post, but whose experience was about the range of a Tommy-gun … few of them had anything really new to say". Slim suggests you trust your instinct. A bad idea, no matter how well presented, is still a bad idea. When choosing what action to take to improve your mental health – beware of the bad idea fairy.

Planning is everything, the plan is nothing. Slim believed that planning was key, particularly with logistics. But he also recognised that things rarely go to plan and that "flexibility of mind" is needed to think your way through, as situations unfold. What is your plan to mental health improvement? Be aware and ready to show "flexibility of mind" when the situation changes.

Keep it short and sweet. Slim warns against information overload. "Anything worth saying, is worth saying briefly". Do not speak endlessly of your health situation, particularly with your spouse/partner. When communicating with health professionals or supporters keep it short and sweet, and then get on with action.

Slim said "Leadership is of the spirit, compounded of personality and vision". Can we use a bit of Bill Slim's leadership magic, born in the atrocious conditions of jungle warfare, to help us lead ourselves to better wellbeing? If so, it starts with having a good plan, but being flexible about it, and limiting discussion about it.

Action: From Slim - Get yourself a good recovery plan, be flexible about it, and limit discussion about it.

"Hero of the past: Gen Slim – don't underestimate having a good plan to turn defeat into victory".

CHAPTER 7: ACTION STATIONS! – RESPOND

Recognise - Recover - Respond

Respond - responses that will directly help you get better.
Chapter summary - in case you prefer to dip in ...

62	Help others - it helps yourself.	Dr Hal Belknap	
63	Recognise the thinking-feeling-doing link. Start feeling better by thinking positive.		
64	Deeds not words - it's the actions you take that change things.	Emily Wilding Davison	
65	Do something to boost your mental health, then go online and talk about it for amplification.		
66	Go neutral - decide not to respond, or just say no.		
67	Surround yourself with disciplined people and be disciplined in your thoughts and disciplined in your actions.		
68	Spit out the 'marbles' because you need to.		
69	Use 'blocking out' in your diary. To rest, recover, think or manoeuvre.		
70	Like BP, use improvisation and creativity to impact both how you feel and how others see you - both helps our health.	Baden Powell	
71	Compartmentalise and time box your work, to allow focus and breaks from your main issue.		
72	Formally and informally share thoughts with your 'band of brothers'.		
73	Ask not how much did I fail, but how much did I learn? Analyse all activity in terms of learning not failure. Learn something new.		
74	Practice 'mindfulness' either as a formal technique or at least be aware of your thoughts and fill your mind FULL of positive thoughts.		

75	Go back to basics - 'bounce hit'. Simplify and strip back to the essential components of good health. Concentrate on getting them right.		
76	Be like Gandhi - disobey your illness.	Mahatma Gandhi	
77	Stay off the drugs unless prescribed by a doctor, and even then view drugs as part of the short term solution not the whole long term solution.		
78	Go for a 'walk and talk' and talk about 'it'.		
79	Speak to your mentor - engage with them more closely.		
80	Step up your nutrition. You are what you eat. Eat more nutritious food.		
81	Count your blessings by making a list that you re-work.		
82	Do what you enjoy - list, diary, action.		
83	Don't own it - you cannot solve a problem that is not yours. Drop the banana.		
84	Actively use the 'garden of the subconscious'.		
85	Do normal things, and track your progress to 'more' normal.		
86	Be open and transparent with others - they will surprise you with how much they can help.		
87	Ask for help, and tell people how they can help.		
88	Accept that you are not alone, you are normal. Reach out and share.		
89	Smile more - it's good for you and for others. It beats the alternative.		
90	'Get a laugh on'. Laugh more. Surround yourself with people who make you laugh. Make others laugh.	Ken Dodd	
91	Move more, and if you can, move more outdoors.		
92	Delegate, abdicate or dump - be sensitive to whether these reduce stress or actually increase stress and for whom.		
93	Go to the dump. Write stuff down. Keep a notebook.		
94	Use urgent and important lists, or do difficult first.		

95	'Graffiti' - express yourself in colour on the wall.		
96	If you are in a tight spot, identify some 'vital mental medicine' - music or entertainment that will raise your spirits.	Ernest Shackleton	
97	Give someone a warm hug or stand them a drink.	Mr Tilley	
98	Get the sand in your toes, the wind on your face, and a fire glow into your eyes.		
99	Keep going, sometimes being free from illness takes a long time.	William Wilberforce	
100	Put things in perspective and do your best to survive the day as best you can.	Alistair Urquhart	

62. Help others – grow yourself.

    One person who created more positive mental health and wellbeing than any other I have known, was American Physician Dr Hal Belknap. Hal was my friend, mentor and fellow Scout Leader. On Hal's death in 2008, 1000 people came to his funeral of all ranks and stations, and people lined the streets of his home town of Norman, Oklahoma. The hospital where he worked emptied of doctors, nurses and patients, stood 3 deep as his cortege passed by and his funeral included a fly past. He was a leader in his church, a leader in Scouting, and a leader as a medical doctor in his community. I was asked to speak at his funeral and like many others who spoke we mentioned his creed and spirit, although interestingly we had not compared notes before, but we all picked up on the same thing. He would say *"there are those in your community who need your help, reach out – helping others is one of the best ways to grow yourself*". He was a superior human being and he was right, helping others with their health actually helps you grow yours! He was always smiling, energetic, enthusiastic and mischievous, a great person to be around. He would be amused that I am writing a manual on health.

    Also in 2008, the New Economics Foundation, identified Five Ways to Wellbeing. The first four are what you might expect: *Connect, Be active, Take notice, Keep Learning*. But the 5th was *Give.* In giving, you help others but you also help yourself.

Further reading: The Five Ways to Wellbeing. New Economics Foundation. 2008.

Some of the research previously mentioned by McGonigal explores that helping others does actually help you reduce your anxiety and help you rise to your challenges, creating resilience, and helps you grow and make you stronger. Ten years after we lost Hal - now medical research shows that helping others does actually change your body chemistry and helps you.

What can you do to help others? It might well be help with their health challenge or it might be help with something completely different. Helping others actually helps you.

Action: Help others – it helps yourself.

"Hero: Hal Belknap – Helping others is one of the best ways to grow yourself".

63. Recognise thinking-feeling-doing link.

We have previously mentioned the danger of thinking that perception is everything. But your thoughts do affect your feelings. In fact your thoughts can change your body chemistry. Thinking positively actually can be a positive outcome as well as part of the process. Positive thoughts can cause physiological changes in your body and make you feel better. This can happen fast. While you will have to deploy this one along with others, a good starting place for your responses is to start positive thinking. Place positive thoughts in your mind and shut out negative ones. We touched upon the impact of the link between the mental and physical earlier, but there is a growing area of science called Neuroplasticity, which accepts that we can rewire our brains. It's not just smoke and mirrors; thoughts can actually change the physical.

Action: Recognise the thinking-feeling-doing link. Start feeling better by thinking positive.

64. Hero of the past - Emily Wilding Davison. Deeds not words.

    Emily Davison 1872-1913 was a militant member of the Woman's Social and Political Union (WSPU), a movement which sought to gain the vote for women on the same basis as men. Her radical actions are closely linked with the women's suffrage movement, but prior to 1918, over a third of the male population had no right to vote either. Democracy in the UK had largely been based on property ownership i.e. wealth. Those unable to vote were criminals, the insane, women and the poor. This included many of the men as well as all the women!

    Emily got up to some unsavoury things, including a hunger strike, violent attack, self-harm while in prison, and bombings, to raise awareness and add political pressure to her cause. She would end her life being knocked down by the King's horse at the 1913 Epsom Derby. On the eve of the 1911 census, Emily hid in a cupboard in the Palace of Westminster so that on the census form she could legitimately give her place of residence that night as the House of Commons! Years later Tony Benn MP, in another act of "deeds not words", and without permission, crept into the cupboard and fixed a plaque on the wall to commemorate the event!

The plaque reads:

IN LOVING MEMORY OF
EMILY WILDING DAVISON

IN THIS BROOM CUPBOARD EMILY WILDING DAVISON HID HERSELF, ILLEGALLY, DURING THE NIGHT OF THE 1911 CENSUS. SHE WAS A BRAVE SUFFRAGETTE CAMPAIGNING FOR VOTES FOR WOMEN AT A TIME WHEN PARLIAMENT DENIED THEM THAT RIGHT.

IN THIS WAY SHE WAS ABLE TO RECORD HER ADDRESS, ON THE NIGHT OF THAT CENSUS, AS BEING "THE HOUSE OF COMMONS", THUS MAKING HER CLAIM TO THE SAME POLITICAL RIGHTS AS MEN.
EMILY WILDING DAVISON DIED IN JUNE 1913 FROM INJURIES SUSTAINED WHEN SHE THREW HERSELF UNDER THE KING'S HORSE AT THE DERBY TO DRAW PUBLIC ATTENTION TO THE INJUSTICE SUFFERED BY WOMEN. BY SUCH MEANS WAS DEMOCRACY WON FOR THE PEOPLE OF BRITAIN.

Notice placed her by Tony Benn MP
"I must tell you, Mr Speaker, that I am going to put a plaque in the House. I shall have it made myself and screwed on the door of the broom cupboard in the Crypt."

Emily's inspiration, and Tony's, is to remind us of the power of having courage to take action. In 1911, the motto for the WSPU was "deeds not words". If in a situation of extreme stress or mental health attack, you can easily spend a lot of time with words not deeds. What actions today and tomorrow will you take to make you better?

"Hero of the past: Emily Wilding Davison – deeds not words".

Action: Deeds not words – it's the actions you take that changes things.

DEEDS ACTION PLAN

	What deeds will I accomplish?	How will this help my Health?
Today		
This week		
This month		
This quarter		

65. Go online – and be liked.

    It's not that the Internet is good or bad, it can be both. The challenge for our generation, and the next is to use it for good, not bad. While social media can be a cause of poor mental health, it can also be something to help. Sending out a tweet, or a post via Linked In / Facebook / Snapchat / Instagram and seeing how many likes or responses you get, can make us feel better. Rather than saying 'don't go online', a better approach is to ask how we can use going online to support our mental health. But be careful. We need to avoid creating a dependency on this, and this becoming part of a self esteem crutch. Just like many socially acceptable drugs, like alcohol and coffee, use in moderation. A cup of coffee a day and a couple of pints of beer a week is good for you. Ten cups of coffee a day and a couple of dozen pints of beer a week, is not. It is likewise with internet 'likes'. Getting "liked" has been shown to release chemicals in us that makes us feel better. While not a substitute to real life and contact, it might be a helpful part of an overall action plan.

Last summer I spent a few days away with my eldest son Ben at the brilliant Edinburgh Comedy Festival, and I tweeted, in three instalments, and posted on Linked In, on World Mental Health Day. Just like the old school activity of showing your holiday snaps to family, a tweet after a good positive mental health experience can amplify the effects. In fact this post has been my most viewed post ever!

Here is the tweet / post:

WORLD MENTAL HEALTH DAY - 7 top tips for leaders: 1. Spend time with someone you love. 2. Give someone a hug. 3. Go to a place where people are laughing and join in (comedy festival). 4. Be kind to someone. 5. Get outside, feel the sun and breeze on your face. 6. Walk and talk. 7. Do all of the above in one day. Picture: With my son Ben at the Edinburgh Fringe this summer. Wonderful!

Action: Do something to boost your mental health, then go online and talk about it for amplification.

66. Go neutral – decide not to respond.

The key thing about a response is that it is a decision. A decision which you actively control. It is not the same as a 'reaction', which you might not consciously control. So you can choose the type of response, the speed, and the severity of the response. You can also choose not to respond; this is a very under-rated technique. It is not the same as not responding through error or omission. A choice of a 'nil response', buys you time; it can stop the situation from escalating; and it can take emotion out of the situation, and give you the sense that you are in control, both of which are good for mental health. The world's greatest investor Warren Buffet, when asked to name one thing that accounted for his success, was reported to have said "say NO!" As managers and leaders we all take on too much, and saying no to the unimportant things buys us the two most important resources, time and energy to focus on the critical things that can really add value.

Action: Go neutral – decide not to respond, or respond by saying no.

67. Good to great - disciplined thoughts and actions.

Whatever of the 100 action points you choose to deploy - you need to proceed in a disciplined way. In one of the most successful management books of recent times Jim Collins sets out how companies can move from "Good" to "Great". The central thread that ran through all the most successful companies was "discipline". Discipline in people, discipline in thought and then discipline in action. Based around extensive research he and his team identified 6 factors on the journey from good to great. Each one of them had discipline at their heart. If we are to breakthrough, reduce our stress and improve health, we must first surround ourselves with disciplined people, and this includes ourselves. Start thinking in a disciplined way, and then take disciplined action. Only then will we breakthrough and start to get better. In today's laissez faire / jeans and T shirt / casual business world, discipline is a very under-rated success ingredient.

Further reading: Good to Great: why some companies make the leap and others don't. Jim Collins. 2001.

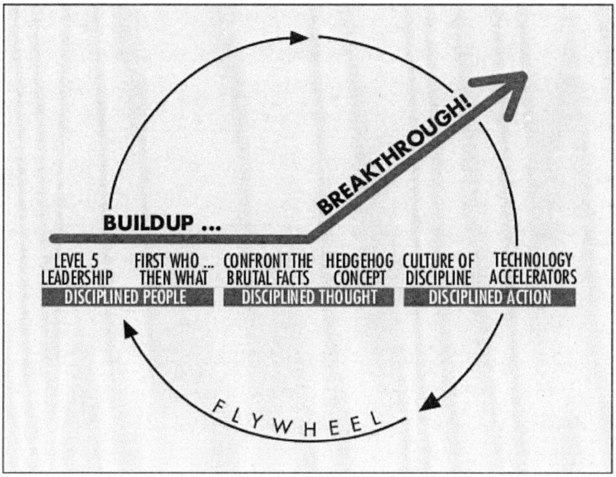

The Flywheel, from Good to Great, Jim Collins 2001.

Mental health and discipline:	Questions:	Score yourself /5	What could you do to improve?
People	How disciplined am I? Am I surrounded by disciplined people to help me?		
Thoughts	Am I avoiding the 13 myths of mental health? Am I thinking positively to help me with: Recognition? Recovery? Reponses?		
Action	Am I deploying many of the 100 action points? Am I sustaining deployment over the long term?		

Action: Surround yourself with disciplined people and be disciplined in your thoughts and disciplined in your actions.

68. Spit out the "marbles" - because you need to.

    On some occasions you need to get things off your chest, simply because you need to say them. In situations such as this, the other person may not be listening or receptive to your points but you will feel better anyway for saying them. This is called 'spitting out the marbles' (from having a mouthful of them). The act of getting them out will help you. Focus on this. Accept that you are unlikely to change the perception of the other person but by saying this stuff you will improve your mental health.

    Action: Spit out the "marbles" - because you need to.

69. Use 'blocking out' in your diary.

    Most of us tend to over-plan and or over-commit to our diaries. This often does not give us the flexibility to respond to the unexpected, or provide sufficient reflection time. One powerful technique is to 'block out' periods of your diary, either with actual activities which allow us rest and recovery or with "dummy meetings" (easily done with electronic dairies). This will mean that you don't get over-full and you have planned in slack time to allow you to rest, recover, think or manoeuvre. It's simple. It works, but it is amazing how many of us don't use this simple tool.

    Action: Use 'blocking out' in your diary. To rest, recover, think or manoeuvre.

70. Hero of the past – Baden Powell – improvise.

    Baden Powell (BP) is known for his creation of the Scout Movement, over 110 years ago. But this was after having completed a first career as a successful soldier. It was the relief of the town of Mafeking in the Second Boer War that catapulted him to national fame. BP was in charge of a small garrison in a town which had been surrounded by the Boers. He was cut off and outnumbered 4 to 1. He held out for an incredible 217 days from October 1899, until relieved. He did this by enlisting the help of all the townspeople, irregular troops, and volunteers, including the cadet corps boys. He employed deception techniques like planting dummy mine fields, and putting up posts to signify barbed wire, when none existed. He moved his limited men and guns around the perimeter, and used a 'homemade' search light. All these measures were designed to signal to the enemy that his defences were stronger than they actually were. At the same time BP, a keen actor himself, organised theatrical productions and sports competitions to keep up morale. His antics were followed by the public back in Britain, reading about the unfolding drama through the newspapers and music hall, as this leader with the X factor "batted on ... not out" day after day.

Although limited in resources, BP knew how the people inside his organisation felt about him, and how those outside it perceived him. He also knew that both these factors were critical in the success of the enterprise. Baden Powell's inspiration is to teach us, no matter how bleak our situation looks, with ingenuity, improvisation and creativity, we can address both the internal morale and external presentation of our situation, and that they feed off each other. As managers of our own health, we need the courage to take action internally and externally for as long as the siege lasts, and until the present stress is relieved. What can you do to boost your morale and communicate to others around you that you are getting better?

Action: Like BP, use improvisation and creativity to impact both how you feel and how others see you to strengthen your health.

"Hero of the past: Robert Baden Powell – improvisation and creativity at Mafeking".

71. Compartmentalise and time box.

Not being able to think about something helps. Switching off from our main concern means that when we return to it we are refreshed, and can also see it from a new angle, or get new insights into it. In fact, returning to a problem, it often seems smaller. Compartmentalising allows you to "park" a problem so that you are not thinking about it. It allows you to enjoy other activities and then return to the problem. Routines help. Techniques for compartmentalising include scribbling on wall charts and segregating the problem by using diagrams; leaving the notes and materials of the issues in a certain place, such as the office; turning the phone off; only actioning at certain times of the day e.g. first 2 hours in the morning. You could also time box, allow a certain amount of time for an activity, say 2 hours - rather than keep going until it you are 100% happy with it. This works well with the 80/20 rule mentioned earlier, as you are unlikely to achieve a lot in the last 20% of your time.

Action: Compartmentalise and time box your work, to allow focus and breaks from your main issue.

72. Better with your "band of brothers".

Most of us feel better when we share things with others. Particularly if we respect and value the opinion of those we work with. Well governed companies have a board. No matter how complex and challenging the situation I have always found that I feel better after having met with the band of brothers / fellow directors. Most leaders take on personal responsibility for things, but sharing them and your concerns with your fellow directors does help share the burden. If you need help, ask them. When I have done this I find, firstly people are more willing to help than you think; they come up with solutions you had not thought of, and you feel great at the end of the encounter. We mentioned before the knights of the round table. This might be a different group than your band of brothers. For me my knights are my personal life-long friends. My band of brothers, are my fellow directors within a certain work situation like a board. It is good to have active support from both groups. I.e. to have both at Action Stations.

Action: formally and informally share thoughts with your "band of brothers".

73. Ask not ... how much did I fail, but ... how much did I learn?

Failure is learning-rich. Anyone doing anything interesting or innovative will fail a lot. In fact all successful journeys are littered with failure along the way. Short term failure is an essential ingredient of long term success. One of the traits of high performance folk in all fields is their attitude to failure. A good day could be one where you learn a lot. The best seek to learn from every aspect of every failure and so move up the hill towards the peak of performance. Many businesses have a blame culture and not a learning culture, which is something Matthew Syed explores in his book 'Black Box Thinking'. One of the best industries for a culture which learns from failure is Aerospace, one of the worst is Health. Where on the scale is your business / industry?

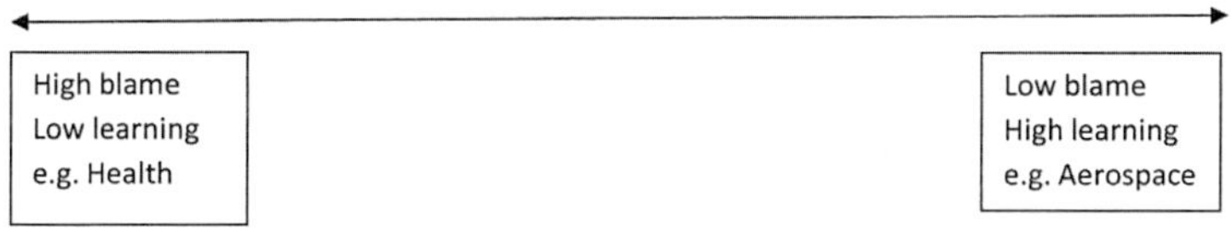

Further reading – Matthew Syed, Black Box Thinking. 2015.

Some think that the process of learning something new can bring therapeutic benefits itself. So aiming to master something new (a sport, a language, an instrument) may be a good strategy in itself.

Action: Ask not how much did I fail, but how much did I learn? Analyse all activity in terms of learning, not failure. Learn something new.

74. Be "mind FULL".

"Mindfulness" is an accepted and helpful wellbeing approach, along with Cognitive Behaviour Therapy (CBT). Although I have not used professional services here, I have used some of the principles. Two of the most powerful principles are the ideas of being aware of your thoughts, and filling your mind with something positive. You cannot simultaneously be thinking about something positive and something negative. A full positive mind does not have room for negative thoughts.

Action: Practise "mindfulness" either as a formal technique or at least be aware of your thoughts and fill your mind FULL of positive thoughts.

75. Go back to basics - bounce hit.

My dad was a keen club tennis player, and shared with us his enthusiasm for sport and for tennis. He would often use the game to teach us, we thought about tennis, but in the lesson would be some useful insights into business and life. He would say - '*some days you will go into the office and things will not go right, like on the court you will mis-time your shots and hit the ball into the net or consistently out of court. Your serve goes to pieces. A weak player lets this lack of form affect them mentally, and this then leads to a worsening of their form'.*

When this happens, and it happens to us all, he would say: *go 'back to basics' and practice 'bounce hit'*. It is the technique of closely watching the ball, when it bounces you say to yourself 'bounce', then you watch it onto your racquet and at the point of impact you say 'hit'. This amazingly simple technique is so powerful to get you hitting the ball well again. It works, we think, because filling your conscious mind with focused thoughts brings your concentration levels up and also prevents negative thoughts. Your subconscious then moves all the muscles and bones and body components to put them in the right position to time the shot. Whatever the theory, it works.

In business if things are going wrong, I often ask myself 'What are the basics?' – let's go back to watching the ball, moving our feet, timing our shots, and with an applied focus on the basics, our form returns. In mental health the basics are often things like sleep, diet, relaxation, thinking positively and surrounding yourself with support. Consider, what are your basics? Review what action you are taking in each of these areas.

Action: Go back to basics – 'bounce hit'. Simplify and strip back to the essential components of good health. Concentrate on getting them right.

76. Hero of the past - Mahatma Gandhi. Disobedience

Mahatma Gandhi was an inspirational leader from India who led millions of people against the British Imperial power in the early part of the twentieth century. Central to Gandhi's approach was peaceful disobedience, an approach that the authorities struggled to respond to. The controlling powers (your stress and illness etc.) expect and predict that you will respond to them in certain ways. Gandhi's inspiration is to teach us that we can choose how we respond. Peaceful disobedience proved even more powerful in changing the course of history for India than armed struggle. View your stress as something that is oppressing you. Your health is your own, but the stress is an external power which you can choose how you respond to. If you are a determined and strong-willed person, adopt Gandhi's view; disobey the stress. Do your own thing in your own time. The human spirit is much more resourceful and resilient than we think.

"Hero of the past: Mahatma Gandhi,
peaceful disobedience".

Action: Be like Gandhi - disobey your illness.

77. Stay off the drugs.

There is a tendency when under stress and mental health attack, to turn to artificial support. This often means excessive alcohol, caffeine, medication, or other drugs. The problem is, they interfere with the body's natural chemicals, making it harder for sustained recovery and can also create a dependency. While drugs can be helpful to relieve pain and stabilise in the short run, be careful to avoid long term or accidental dependency. If you are to go with drugs, do so under medical supervision, and view them as temporary help. Be aware of accidental increases in drug use, for example a few extra alcoholic drinks at the end of the day or a few extra cups of coffee. Often use can creep up without us being consciously aware of it. Periodically audit your drug use and with your doctor have an appropriate plan.

Action: Be aware of the role that drugs can play. As a general rule, stay off drugs, unless prescribed by a doctor; even then view drugs as part of the short term solution not the whole long term solution.

78. Go for a 'walk and talk', and talk about "it".

    Previously we talked about going for a 'walk and talk', and NOT talking about "it". In this section I ask you to consider a 'walk and talk', and talk about it. In fact both are good and even better when used in the same week. Walking is very therapeutic. Not only is it good for our bodies, it helps release thoughts and relaxes the mind. Our grandparents were right, fresh air is good for you. Sometimes telling someone on a walk what is on your mind and dumping every detail of what your concerns are, is very helpful. It helps if you can walk in a beautiful place. Some of my mentoring for leaders takes place on walks on the North Norfolk Coast. Choose carefully who partners you in the 'walk and talk about 'it''. Your spouse/partner might not be the best person.

    Action: Go for a 'walk and talk', and talk about 'it'.

"Nelsonspirit Peer Mentoring - walking and talking with your peers in a beautiful place".

79. Speak to your mentor.

    Speak with your mentor. Every leader should have one. If you don't have one, get one. A good mentor can provide intellectual challenge and emotional support. They can be a critical friend, devoid of the emotional baggage that comes with people who are emotionally close to us, such as our family. Mentoring differs from coaching in that mentors let the mentee (recipient) lead the agenda and the interaction is non-directive. Both these aspects make mentoring a good vehicle to provide health support. If you are in a tight spot, consider meeting your mentor more frequently. If you normally see them monthly, change it to fortnightly or weekly. If a mentee actually tells their mentor they are not coping or are under extreme stress then engage the power of the mentor to help. Giving the mentor the 'heads up' in advance of the meeting also helps. Good mentors are usually very good listeners. It also helps if the mentor has themselves been through extreme stress in their business career, and so can talk from personal experience.

    Action: Speak to your mentor – engage with them more closely.

80. Step up your nutrition – you are what you eat.

    The quality of the food we eat is very important. So much of the discourse (noise) around food is based on the quantity of what we eat rather than the quality. The narrative is usually around calories and dieting. Quality of food intake is nutrition. Good nutrition means that we feel good, we get energy and vitality, our body repairs itself and releases good chemicals into our bodies. When under extreme stress our defence systems are eroded, and resources depleted. Good nutrition is a great way to restore balance and full operating capacity for us. Eat a balanced diet with plenty of unprocessed and fresh food, especially fruit and vegetables. One small thing you can do when under health attack is tilt the balance in your diet and improve it. Be careful not to make a diet an obsession otherwise it might become a stressor. More books have been written on diets than I have had hot dinners, but here are a few of my favourite one liners:

You are what you eat.
The best diet is a balanced diet.
Fast food, fast to illness.
The best diet is a natural diet – avoid processing.
The best diet is a diet full of colour.
Food gives you energy, nutrition keeps you well.

Action: Step up your nutrition. You are what you eat. Eat more nutritious food.

81. Count your blessings.

We often undervalue the things we have and overvalue the things we do not have. Consciously reviewing all the things you have which are good does help. Make the list or have it as an agenda item on your walk and talk. Make a list now of all the things that you are lucky to have and all the good aspects of your situation. Dwell and reflect on that list. Repeat this activity in a few days and see if you can make the list longer. If that works, repeat.

Action: Count your blessings by making a list that you re-work.

82. Do what you enjoy.

When we are under high levels of work stress and mental health attack, we tend to cope by working longer hours. Often things that we enjoy get squeezed out. Make a list of the top 10 things you enjoy. When did you last do each of them? 'Diary' to do them in the short run. If you can stop the things you do not enjoy, do so. If one is your employment situation that you cannot extract yourself from short term, resolve to exit from it in the long run. Grab 5 minutes and think about the things you really enjoy doing. Ask yourself when you last did them. Plan a date to do them again.

	The 10 things I enjoy the most:	Date last did it?	Plan for action - commit to a time and place.
1			
2			
3			
4			
5			
6			
7			
8			
9			
10			

Action: Do what you enjoy – list, diary, action.

83. Don't own it - you cannot solve a problem that is not yours – drop the banana.

This is a tale of how you catch a monkey, some say from Colonial India, others from Colonial Africa. Bananas are placed in bamboo cages just big enough for the monkey to put their hands through, but not big enough for the monkey to extract their hand holding a banana. Monkeys attracted by the smell and sight of the banana would force their hands through the cage and try to seize one. They were then caught by man. The monkeys did not have the wit to spring their escape. All they had to do was drop the banana and then they could remove their hand from the cage, run off and avoid capture. As leaders we all hold onto bananas, issues and problems that we won't let go. These often manifest themselves as problems that you do not own, they are not yours. Are you holding any bananas? Most of us are. You will never be able to solve them. We all go around collecting bananas, worrying about a whole load of stuff that we can do very little (anything) about. These bananas end up trapping us, and we end up with something bad happening, and we don't even get to eat the bananas. If you are not going to be able to get the banana, drop it.

List of my bananas (things I cannot control or exert little influence over and I would be better to drop them):

Name of the banana (the problem):	Drop it by:

Action: Don't own it - you cannot solve a problem that is not yours. Drop the banana.

84. Actively use the 'garden of the subconscious'.

Our brains have two parts: the conscious, where we are aware of our thoughts; and the subconscious, which is what goes on behind the scenes. The conscious is the tip of the iceberg and scientists tell us that most of our thinking power goes on in the subconscious. This is when we are asleep or while we are consciously thinking of different things. Just to compare, scientists believe the conscious (what we are aware we are thinking) can hold up to 80 thoughts per second, but the subconscious works at a speed of 11 million thoughts per second.

Many believe that worry is when the subconscious floods our conscious with things we have not done. The evidence is that thoughts planted in the subconscious grow; these thoughts can be positive or negative. *"I have not started that report yet and it is due in next Tuesday"*, is a negative thought and your subconscious will keep reminding your conscious of this. The subconscious needs to work on something, recognise this. Rather than let it be the harvester of worry, plant positive thoughts in it and let it work on them. Some view the subconscious as a garden; whatever seed or thought you plant, it will grow. It is natural for your subconscious mind to work on things, like it is natural for weeds to appear in your garden. Plant positive seeds and then you will harvest positive thoughts. The earlier you plant the positive thoughts, the longer your subconscious has to work on them. I know many leaders who prepare for work by allocating 10 minutes a day of conscious time to move a project along. *"I will just make a note of this (+) great idea (+), in my notebook (+) and it will help shape (+) the presentation that I am looking forward to doing (+) next week, which I am ahead of schedule with in relation to my planning (+)"*. Actively using the natural working of the subconscious can be very powerful. With mental health, plant positive seeds, and avoid negative ones.

Action: Actively use the 'garden of the subconscious'.

85. Do normal things.

When you or your partner are under extreme stress or mental health attack, you tend to stop doing normal things. You become physically or mentally unable to cope with them. This comes along with falling confidence and falling energy levels. Normal things include: seeing friends, going to the cinema, doing your hobbies, going to the local shops, housework, riding a bike. As you cut these things out you can become increasingly concerned that you are not able to do them. This is common if you are spiralling down the curve identified in phase 3, back in Chapter 2. One thing that really helped Nicki and I, was to have in our recovery strategy a line entitled "Normalisation". I.e. we are going to slowly and progressively do normal things. At month-end you can look back and say 'this month we have been able to do X, which we could not do the month before, so we are making progress'. Normal (or well) is the opposite to ill. So the more normal things you can do, the more well you can prove to yourself you are.

Action: Do normal things, and track your progress to 'more' normal.

86. Be open and transparent with others.

    I have found the more open and transparent you are with others about your health, the better. Most people in life are nice and want to help. If we let people know that we need help, in most cases, they respond. It is what community is all about. This seems to work, whether the other people are known to you or not.

    Action: Be open and transparent with others; they will surprise you with how much they can help.

87. Ask for help.

    Sometimes it is useful to go even further than just being open and transparent. Sometimes it is useful to ask for help. *"I am not coping and I need help"* can be very powerful, especially if you are the sort of person who does not normally say this. Many people might say to you *"If I can be any help, just let me know"*. It can be useful to have an answer lined up for this – *"yes thank you, you can be of great help – if you did XX"*. At which point you have just recruited another volunteer to your recovery team!

    Action: Ask for help, and tell people how they can help.

88. Accept that you are not alone; you are normal. Reach out and share.

    Many illnesses, particularly mental health ones, can be accompanied by an element of loneliness. Sometimes the more the person is a leader or in control before the mental health deterioration, the worse this can be. Recognise that this is normal. Also accept that many other people have a mental health problem, in fact most of us do. Reach out to others, help them and ask for their help. It starts by accepting that you are not alone and sharing your story. A great example of this is Princes William and Harry speaking out about their mental health challenges. Mental health affects us all, as Kipling said, 'Coachman and Kings'. Everyone from the most junior to the most senior person in your organisation has mental health, and at times, this will not be good. Sharing can help you and inspire others.

Action: Accept that you are not alone, you are normal. Reach out and share.

89. Smile more.

Such a simple one. When we smile, we feel better and we make others feel better. Smiling projects sunshine and love. Smiling is part of the clothes we wear and the messages we project. When we "dress up" we feel more the part. Likewise with smiling. You might only be acting the part of being happy, but it does help. Remember others will be worried about your mental health: if you smile you are helping to improve both your mental health and theirs.

I keep fit by playing sport, swimming and running. I run around my local village once or twice a week. On my set route I used to pass a man in a wheelchair who had parked it at the end of his drive. He would sit there in the evenings and wave to the traffic. People got to know he was there and they would wave back, and regulars would hoot their horns. Like others I would wave at him each time I passed and he would always smile at me and I would smile back. After this had happened a number of times I eventually did the very un-British thing and stopped to ask this stranger his name. He smiled and said "My name's John". I said "John can I ask you a question? Every time I run past you are smiling and everyone who sees you smiles back – why is this?" He said "well ... **that beats the alternative**". We both laughed and as I completed my run that night, I reflected that the man in the wheel chair had just taught me a lesson about mental health and about life. Smiling is good - and it beats the alternative.

Action: Smile more – it's good for you and for others. It beats the alternative.

90. "Get a laugh on".

The only thing better than smiling is laughing. I'm not sure where I heard it but a leader once told me that "laughing is a spontaneous expression of life". It makes us feel good. It is one of the first things that comes into a relationship that this maturing and growing, and one of the first things to leave when a relationship is under stress. How much do you laugh? Who do you laugh with? People like being with people who make them laugh. We often measure the success of a social situation by the phrase "it was a good laugh". Laughing cuts across creeds, cultures, genders, race etc, as long as of course we are laughing with, as opposed to, at. By including someone in the joke, you are showing respect. And we English do enjoy laughing at ourselves. It is no surprise that in some of the most demanding and stressful work environments like the military, laughter is usually present in spades. Chat, banter, craic, mickey taking, it has many names. It underpins brotherhood and camaraderie. One of the things that ex-servicemen say when they leave the services is they miss this narrative of mutual support. I believe, the role laughing plays in mental health is extremely underrated. Of course it can be a challenge to laugh when you are in the depths of a mental health condition. But I would like to borrow advice from Eddie Braburn, the scriptwriter for Morecombe and Wise, who told the boys who were concerned about the bed routine he had written for them: "if it's good enough for Laurel and Hardy, it's good enough for you". My thought is that if banter is good enough for the Military, it's good enough for you. We all have different favourite comedians; one of mine was Ken Dodd. He spread so much happiness to others in his life.

Action: "Get a laugh on". Laugh more. Surround yourself with people who make you laugh. Make others laugh.

"Hero: Ken Dodd – King of Laughter".

91. Move more.

Not all of us are able to control our diaries to the extent that playing sport every day is realistic, but all of us can control how much we move. One simple tool is to consider how much we move, and move more. Kinetic learning is the idea that we learn best when we are moving. So why not apply this to health? Walk to the bus; walk up the stairs etc. Moving is generally good for us, especially outdoors. Walking, cycling, swimming all plug into this. Moving not only burns off calories, it makes us feel better too. There is also something magical connecting movement to the brain. Movement generates all sorts of feel-good chemicals.

Action: Move more, and if you can, move more outdoors.

92. Delegate, abdicate or dump.

Everyone is now 'too busy'. When you ask business people how they are, the word 'busy' often appears in their answer. But as one of my mentors taught me "busyness" can be the enemy of "business!". Activity or busyness which leads to an illusion of progress, and often self-importance, is not the same as Action, which leads to profitability and adds value. So the first question to ask yourself is: are you engaged in activity or action? It is true that the information revolution impacts all our lives, there is more and more to be done, and often much more to be done than time available to do it. So how do we cope with this challenge? One of the classic ways to reduce workload is to use delegation. But be careful, good delegation to followers often requires MORE of your time to brief, counsel, coach, explain, monitor, and review. Delegation can often take more of your time and can create stress! Also be careful about abdicating: this is where you pass work to followers but do not provide them with the necessary support. This too can often lead to higher levels of stress for you and them too. Dumping is much better. Actively decide it's not going to happen and chuck it all in the bin. Encourage your followers to dump; this actively relieves their stress too. But be careful, you are not just moving the stress from one part of your organisation to another.

Action: Delegate, abdicate or dump – be sensitive to whether these reduce stress or actually increase stress and for whom.

93. Go to the dump - write stuff down.

    There is another form of dumping. Rather than in the bin, this one is where you download your thoughts onto paper. It's another very under-rated technique. Younger leaders are missing out on this old school approach as we move to a paperless world. It's simple ... grab a pen and paper (pencil for really 'old school'), and pour out all your thoughts onto the paper. Brain maps are best, or if you prefer, lists. When I am under extreme stress I keep a pen and paper by my bedside to capture thoughts at night. I have also found it useful to carry a notebook on me and at the point in the day when I am "ambushed" by thoughts relating to the problem, either positively or negatively, I write them down. I also take my notebook on family holidays and capture any ideas I have when relaxing, good and bad. This allows me to capture but not invest time, so I can enjoy the holiday, but know they are recorded so I can come back to them. When you come back to them on return to work, they never seem as scary as when you first had them, and also your subconscious has been working on solutions ever since you captured the thoughts.

    Action: Go to the dump. Write stuff down. Keep a notebook.

94. 'Urgent and important' lists or 'do difficult first'.

    Sometimes writing things down is enough. If your list is long, you might like to mark against each point to prioritise or order the items. A regular ranking list can do this or you could use the classification: U (Urgent) and M (Important). The thinking being that if you are strict with this, you will find that things are never as urgent or important as you first thought. If you do this every day, you can re-rank and you have a very simple but effective management tool. The conventional wisdom is that you do the high Us and Ms first. I was recently on a leadership programme at St George's House, Windsor Castle, where I am Fellow, and Admiral Sir James Nugent RN (RTD) challenged this. His point was that in today's complex world, if you are surrounded by a capable team, most things the leader sees are both urgent and important. He said that he tended to do the most difficult first. I have tried James' idea - it works.

Important but not urgent (M)	Urgent and important (U&M)
Neither important nor urgent	Urgent and not important (U)

Classify tasks into this boxes, and then ring the difficult ones, and do these first.

Action: Use urgent and important lists, or do difficult first.

95. "Graffiti" – fill the wall.

One variation of the 'dump it' technique is to use the sticky flip chart sized paper that you can position on the wall. You use pens that can be erased. It is a good way to get out your thoughts from mapping out, to an action plan. It has the advantage over pen and paper in that you can use movement and be more dramatic as you write things on the wall. You can also remove things by rubbing out and when they cease to be a problem or take the whole thing down and throw it away. Colour helps too. While all this might seem child's play, the process of getting out your thoughts and ordering them and then consigning output to a bin does work.

Action: "Graffiti" – express yourself in colour on the wall.

96. Hero of the past – Shackleton "Vital Mental Medicine".

The Imperial Trans-Antarctic Expedition 1914-17, was led by the great Edwardian explorer Ernest Shackleton. In 1916, Shackleton's ship got stuck on the ice flow and he then led one of the greatest survival and rescue adventures of all time, getting everyone home safely. When his ship, the Endurance, was stuck on the ice, Shackleton let every man take off the ship only a few items of a few pounds (in weight) for the forthcoming survival trek. He made an exception for one item, the banjo, brought by the ship's meteorologist, Hussey. Shackleton said it was needed as it would be "Vital Mental Medicine". Shackleton knew that the survival journey would be demanding, both mentally and physically, and that keeping morale high would be critical. Having a banjo with them could provide hours of morale-lifting entertainment. He was proved right.

"Shackleton's men"

Music can be a great healer. Listening to or playing music is therapeutic. This could be actively listening, which requires concentration, using it as a wind-down routine to get to sleep, or passively listening while you go about other things. Listen to what you like. Get some music in your life; it will cheer you up. Entertaining others can also be uplifting. Being in a band or a concert party, or collectively putting on a performance is a sure way to a laugh. Each of Shackleton's men could entertain by doing something. Interestingly Hussey was not the world's greatest musician but Shackleton recognised that playing the banjo would be his 'party piece' and if each man could entertain the others each evening, morale could be maintained. What is your vital mental medicine? How can you get more music in your life?

Action: If you are in a tight spot, identify some 'vital mental medicine' - music or entertainment that will raise your spirits.

"Hero of the past: Ernest Shackleton – 'We must have the banjo, it's Vital Mental Medicine' ".

97. Give somebody a warm hug.

    It's nearly 10 years now since I purchased my Tilley Hat, made in Canada by outdoors people for outdoors people. It has been one of the best pieces of clothing I have ever purchased. Each hat comes with some "Brag Tags", raffle ticket type cards inside the hat for you to give out to others. They contain the following wording:

    "Most Tilley Hat wearers, and the person beside you is a prime example, are interesting people of sterling character. It is well worth cultivating their acquaintance! To that end, you'll be pleased to learn it is customary to provide the giver of a Tilley Hat procurement information with A WARM HUG, OR STAND HIM OR HER TO A DRINK."

    Canadian "warm hug" = English "cuddle". A few years ago I was waiting in a queue in Disneyland Florida with my family. I spotted a man wearing a Tilley Hat. Having confirmed it was a Tilley, and that we both knew about Brag Tags, we spontaneously gave each other a hug and bought each other a drink. We have no connection with Tilley other than we are satisfied customers, and we were insiders to a fun story.

    I like being described as someone who is interesting and of sterling character and I like that idea of meeting others who are!

I like being on the inside of a joke. I know it's ridiculous. It's a hat. It's all made up. We all know that. But our mental health and that of those with us soared that day. Ever since, I have realised that giving someone a cuddle, buying them a drink, being on the inside of a joke, or wearing your favourite clothing, can raise your mental health and the mental health of others! Thank you Mr Tilley.

Action: Give someone a warm hug or stand them a drink.

"Hero: Mr Tilley with his hats"

98. Earth, wind and fire.

    If you are looking for a fast fix as opposed to a slow burn, here are three things guaranteed to make you feel better: go for walk on a beach; feel the wind on your face; and stare into a real fire. I don't know why but all three seem to have magical properties. If you can do all three in one day, and then pour yourself your favourite drink to celebrate, then give someone you love a cuddle – and we are well on our way!

    Action: Get the sand in your toes, the wind on your face, and a fire glow into your eyes.

99. Hero of the past – William Wilberforce. Keep going.

    William Wilberforce (1759-1833) was a statesman and reformer. He was a leading light in the abolition of the slave trade. In the late 18th Century the slave trade was big business.

Many people were making a lot of money out of it and ports such as Liverpool and Bristol owed their prosperity to it. In a triangular trade model, products such as guns and cloth were sent to West Africa, and were traded for slaves. These were shipped to the West Indies and America to work on plantations, in exchange for products such as sugar, tobacco and rum, for return to Britain. The uncomfortable fact is, that many (most?) people of the time thought this to be a normal and legitimate business. Wilberforce was driven by his Christian principles and set off on a personal mission to abolish the slave trade. There were hundreds of wealthy and powerful people who would lose out if the trade was abolished and they would fight fiercely to defend what they saw as their lucrative and acceptable business. Wilberforce had to submit his abolition of slavery bill to parliament on 12 separate occasions before it was finally accepted. He made his first speech on the matter in 1789. He submitted his bill in 1791, and it was defeated; 1792 – gradual abolition agreed in principle but without timetable; 1805 passed in the Commons but failed in the Lords. In fact it was not until 1807, 18 years after his first speech, that he succeeded. He suffered 12 major setbacks over 18 years before breakthrough.

Wilberforce's inspiration is to remind us that our journey might take far longer than we have planned to reach success in health. As Nelson Mandela was to prove centuries later, the walk to freedom is often a long one. Health is being free from illness. Keep going.

Action: Keep going; sometimes being free from illness takes a long time.

"Hero of the past – William Wilberforce, 12 rejections over 18 year before slavery abolished."

100. Hero of the past – Alistair Urquhart. Survive the day.

I would like to leave the last word on action to one of my granddad's generation.

Alistair Urquhart was conscripted into the British army in 1939. At the age of 19 he was posted to Singapore, where he took part in one of the worst military defeats in British history. The embarrassment of defeat and capture by the Japanese was compounded when they were crowded into Changi prison, and kept in vile conditions. He was then put in a blisteringly hot cattle wagon and transported for 5 days into the jungle, with hardly any room to breathe, sleeping and defecating standing up. Some died on the trip but Alistair survived. At the end of the line, he was made to trek through the jungle for another 5 days, with colleagues who were too ill or weak, bayoneted and left to die. At the camp, they were used as slave labour to build the bridge over the River Kwai. For the next year he would suffer malnutrition, dehydration, fatigue, cholera, cruelty and torture at the hands of his guards. Many died but Alistair survived. In 1943 he thought his lot was going to improve. He was put on a ship to be taken to Japan – but this was torpedoed by a US submarine, unaware of its cargo. Jumping into burning oil, he swam from the ship and drifted on a single man raft for five days without food or water, going temporarily blind. His luck seemed to have changed when he was finally picked up by a passing ship ... but this turned out to be Japanese! He was then put ashore near a small fishing village of ... Nagasaki. Shortly after he arrived it had an atomic bomb dropped on it. Many died. Alistair survived.

After 3½ yrs of malnutrition, dehydration, capture, illness, torture, sinking and having an atomic bomb dropped on him ... what can he teach us? He modestly said that luck played a part in his survival, but he also says you make your own luck. Every day he had one objective - to 'survive the day'. He also said, the hardest thing was coming home and feeling that nobody cared. Alistair's inspiration and that of the 'forgotten army', reminds us to put our troubles in perspective, and focus on doing today's business today. As today's leaders we owe our respect and thanks to Alistair and his friends. They also remind us that the greatest asset of any business or community is the care we have for each other. If we remember this they will not be forgotten.

On the days when my own stress and mental health were not great - I thought of Alistair and how much worse his challenges were, and this helped me get through the day.

Further reading: The Forgotten Highlander: My Incredible Story of Survival During the War in The Far East. Alistair Urquhart. 2011.

Action: Put things in perspective and do your best to survive the day as best you can.

PART THREE:
STRESS AND LEADERSHIP

CHAPTER 8: BASE CAMP FOR LEADERS

Base Camp is somewhere safe, where we prepare for the adventures that lie ahead. Where we get ourselves ready mentally and physically for our journey. Base camp for leaders is where we can check our OWN mental health. If we are to achieve outstanding performance and help our followers with their performance and mental health, we need to first make sure that our own health is in order.

Leaders come in all shapes and sizes, from all backgrounds. As the great leadership expert Warren Bennis says, there are as many definitions of leadership as people you ask. Although it might be difficult to define, we know it when we see it.

Having worked with hundreds of leaders from all sectors around the world, having studied leadership, and tried to practise leadership, I have concluded that of this very eclectic group, one of the few things that the best leaders have in common, is that they elicit great performance out of themselves and importantly from those that choose to follow them. I believe leadership is the magic that inspires others to great performance. When it comes to mental health, there are some differences across sectors and across cultures. Interestingly leaders in the public service and charity sector appear to be the weakest at diagnosing and maintaining their own health. They tend to give away all their energy to look after their followers and sometimes there is nothing left in the tank to support themselves. Their "give away" is high.

All leaders are under stress most of the time. In fact anyone who is trying to perform will have a certain level of stress; it goes with the territory. Most of the time we will be OK, this is normal, and we have normal responses to deal with this (revisit chapter 2). But occasionally we will come under MENTAL HEALTH ATTACK ... and when this happens, or ideally before it happens, we need to GET TO ACTION STATIONS! My argument is that given the information-based world we live in, these attacks are likely to increase in both frequency and severity.

I would like to recap on some suggested approaches to help you establish how well you are dealing with your own stress.

HOW SEVERE IS THE STRESS/MENTAL HEALTH ATTACK?

As a leader you will need to decide whether the situation requires you and your followers to get to Actions Stations or not. The key to this is making an assessment about whether you are under **excessive and sustained** stress, I will call this **XStress.** Are you under XStress?

XStress is where you are under severe and sustained stress, (a mental health attack) and this could lead to a mental health deterioration.

The decision here has three outcomes. Are you under XStress?

A) NO - no further action required.

B) NO - but I'm going to Get to ACTION STATIONS! anyway.

C) YES - Get to ACTION STATIONS!

You might like to plot your stressors, or disruptors of mental health into the following box:

Not sustained, but SEVERE.	SUSTAINED and SEVERE.
Not sustained or severe.	SUSTAINED and Not severe.

Alternatively, in order to help you decide whether you are at XStress we can revisit some models we looked at earlier:

The stress equation (Chapter 3).
The mental health continuum or spectrum (Chapter 3).
Mental health fitness (Chapter 3).

Mental health ladder (Chapter 3).
The "All Blacks" (Chapter 4).

THE STRESS EQUATION (CHAPTER 3).

$$\beta\,(P \times D) > (B \times C)\ 1/\beta$$

We feel stressed when P x D is greater than B x C, i.e. when our perceived demands of the situation are greater than our believed capability to safely deal with the situation. And this is multiplied up or down, depending on whether we perceive the stress to be helpful or harmful (β).

If the left hand side of this equation is excessively and consistently greater than the right hand side - you are in XStress. Are you in XStress?

THE MENTAL HEALTH CONTINUUM OR SPECTRUM (CHAPTER 3)

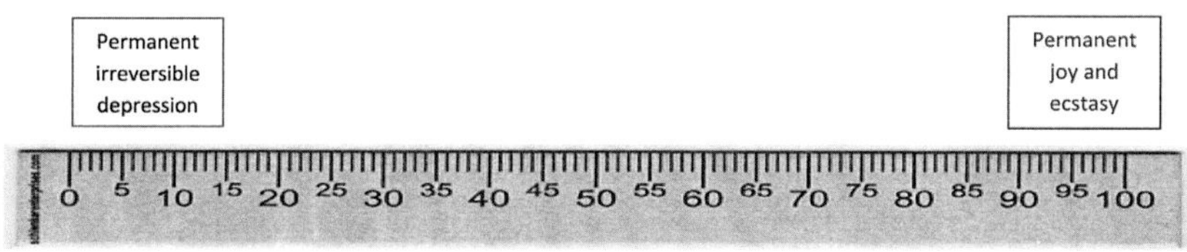

Plot your own mental health somewhere on this range using:

Title:	Serious condition	Not well / struggling to cope	Normal range	Very fit/well for an amateur	Elite fitness/ wellness for an athlete
Normal parlance:	Mental Health condition	Mental health problem	Distress - stress	Eustress	In the elite zone
Performance features:	Long term off work.	Short term off Work.	Average performance.	Good performance	Elite performance
Typical dispostion:	Can't face work.	Hate going in.	Good days and bad.	Liking it	Loving it
Typical medication:	On multiple medications.	On medication.	Self medicate with non presciption drugs (tablets, coffee, alcohol, etc).	None (other than sport or hobbies).	None (extreme engagement in sport or hobbies).

	☹☹☹	☹☹	☹	☺	☺☺	☺☺☺
Your position on the continuum?	0-20 XStress	21-40 XStress	41-60		61-80	81-100
Where do you score?						

If you score less than 40, you are in XStress. Are you in a XStress?

MENTAL HEALTH FITNESS (CHAPTER 3).

Think like an athlete, not like patient.

	Meaning in mental health	How fit are you? Your score /10? XStress is <5
Mental power / strength	The size of the positive thoughts you have?	
Mental speed	How many positive thoughts do you have per minute?	
Mental mobility / agility	The speed (per minute) that you turn negative thoughts into positive?	
Mental stamina	The length of period you can sustain negative thoughts and deal with them?	

If, on average, you are scoring less than 5, you are in XStress. Are you in XStress?

MENTAL HEALTH LADDER (CHAPTER 3).

Where on the ladder are you?

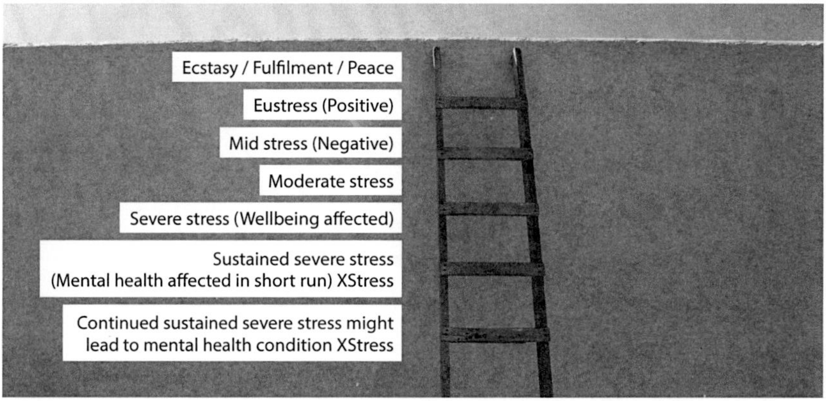

Photo Credit: © Mikołaj Bleja. Licensed by Pexels (www.pexels.com)

If you are on a rung lower than "severe stress" - you are in XStress. Are you in XStress?

THE "ALL BLACKS"(CHAPTER 4).

Let's revisit the 'All Black' list and tick off any that are pertinent to you.

1	Death and bereavement.	
2	Illness of a close family member or self.	
3	Concern over the wellbeing of a child or parent.	
4	Concern over the wellbeing of spouse/partner.	
5	Concern over the wellbeing of self.	
6	Relationship issues with a child or parent.	
7	Relationship issues with a spouse/partner.	
8	You or partner having an affair.	
9	Risk of losing your job/major contract.	
10	Risk of legal action against you.	
11	Risk of your reputation/good name/character being attacked.	
12	Business merger, takeover, sale, cessation or change in ownership.	

13	Business cash flow difficulties.	
14	Personal cash flow difficulties.	
15	Worry about not having enough money in the medium or longer term.	
16	Concern over relationship with boss.	
17	Having to deal with more and more work on less and less resource.	
18	Culture at work has changed for the worse – not like it used to be.	
19	Concern with the relationship with a major customer or supplier.	
20	Relationship with a powerful individual at work (bullying or power games).	
21	Comparison with others – I/we are falling behind, socially or financially.	
22	Non-acceptance or lack of recognition by your peers.	
23	Mid-life crisis – a search for meaning and purpose.	
24	Life event cross road – e.g. child birth or children leaving the nest.	
25	Concern that you are trapped on medication and can't get off it.	
26	Addictive behaviours (drugs, alcohol, sex, medication).	
27	Long term unhappiness with life.	
28	Concern that you are always tired.	
29	Sleep problems.	
30	Boredom – not enough challenge.	
31	Your spouse/partner/girlfriend/boyfriend scoring 2 or more of the above.	
32	Your spouse/partner/girlfriend/boyfriend scoring 4 or more of the above	
	Others ... not mentioned above	
	Others ... not mentioned above	
	Others ... not mentioned above	
	How many do you face? XStress is >2	

If you face 3 or more "All blacks" you are in XStress. Are you in a XStress?

SUMMARY

Are you are under stress? Normality check ... most leaders are!

Are you under severe and sustained stress i.e. 'XStress'? Is the left hand side of the stress equation dominant? Are you are <40 on the mental health continuum? Is your mental fitness <5? Are you on the sustained severe stress rung of the mental health ladder? Do you face more than 2 'All Blacks'?

If you are at XStress - get to ACTION STATIONS! Go to the Appendix now and commit to which of the 100 points you will deploy. Create an action plan.

If you are not at the point of XStress, that's fine. But you may still want to take action. Writing this book has itself inspired me to see if I can lift and maintain my own mental health, which is now much better, in the elite range. So even if you are not under mental health attack currently and might not be at XStress, you can still deploy the Action Stations points. Finally, you might want to consider how you can help your followers through this exercise.

Base camp for leaders is where we can check our OWN mental health. The better your own mental health, the greater your capacity to lead well. Spend some time in base camp making sure your mental health is maintained and improved, and that you are fit to lead

CHAPTER 9: ACTIONS FOR LEADERS STRESS BUSTERS AND MENTAL HEALTH BOOSTERS

This chapter is about what you can do to help with the stress, mental health and performance of your followers. It contains 15 Actions that can be used as **stress busters or mental health boosters.** They do not replace sustainable great leadership but might be something a good leader can add to their toolkit to deploy fast, if their followers are under mental health attack.

One of the magical aspects of leadership is that the leader has within their gift, a capacity to rapidly increase or decrease the stress of their followers by their actions. Over the years I have witnesses some outstanding leaders galvanise, enthuse, excite and charge-up their followers in times of stress. The interesting thing is when I have seen this happen, it usually helps boost the mental health of the leader, as well as their followers. In fact, some would say that the real test of leadership comes when the followers are most stressed and turn to the leader for direction, and inspiration.

Before we explore, I need to make the point that one of the most important things in leadership is authenticity. While the strategies below can be viewed as approaches and techniques, if deployed, they must come across as natural for the leader, and be delivered in the leader's own style, otherwise followers will think they are being 'played' and this is a guaranteed turn off!

The first two actions to bust stress and boost mental health, relate directly to the 100 ACTION STATIONS! points. This manual has been written for the leader or performer to use on themselves. Obviously the actions can be shared with others to help them. Here are the first two:

1. Deploy 100 ACTION STATIONS! for you, and make this visible to your followers. Recognize that you are under mental health

attack, tell your followers and tell them what you are doing to deal with the situation. In this way you ignite the leadership fire of EXAMPLE.

2. ENCOURAGE your followers to Deploy 100 ACTION STATIONS! for themselves. How you do this will be unique to you, and vary by context, culture and capabilities of your followers, but they will need to take ownership of the action points, if they are to be of real value to them. Sheep dipping them will not work.

Although the following strategies touch on some of the ACTION STATIONS! points, they are worth expanding further:

3. TURN UP (AND SAY SOMETHING). One of the strongest things a leader can do when the troops/workers are under high stress is to turn up in the front line. This might be a general in a battlefield, or a head teacher in a classroom, or the MD of the business on the production line. If you do this when they, and you, are busiest, it sends a strong signal and a mental health boost to the troops. Make a speech if that is your style and if appropriate. Show some interest in the lower echelons, and when you are gone, this will spread like a wild fire and warm the hearts of those at the coal face. When things get tough, people need leadership, and the comfort of knowing that there is someone who is running things who they have confidence in, and who has confidence in them.
4. HAVE A PLAN. In every type of organisation I have ever worked, ranging from the military, to a school, to a business, to a government department, to a university; people always doubt whether "they" (the people in charge), know what they are doing. Often the people at the front end either don't know what the plan is, or don't believe in it, let alone know what they have to do to move things forward. Plans get out of date so fast, particularly with the speed of new information. If you ask staff to say what the plan is, most usually do not know, and some choose to believe that the leaders don't actually have a plan. Get a plan. Even if you have to change it every day. Provide the followers with confidence that you have a plan and the ability to adjust it and create a new plan. During one corporate recovery I led, we identified 42 action points that needed to be done in order, and these would take us 3 months. We monitored

them every week, crossing off the ones that were done and re-ordering the others. It was amazing how the stress levels fell and mental health rose as we cracked on through the list. By working the plan as Chairman, I was able to give structure and discipline to our actions. We delivered the plan in full, ahead of schedule.

5. MOMENTUM. It is the nature of groups that gossip and morale spread in spirals up, and down. If the leader can create forward momentum, by lifting morale or following through when mental health is raised, then this can amplify things and make things go faster. With two bits of good news the same day, the second is always received with more merit than it warrants. You can create momentum as a leader by making sure positive things are followed through quickly with other positive things. 'Quick wins' are always a good way of getting this going.
6. NARRATIVE. Just like Action point 1 when we spoke about Googling your personal soundtrack, the leader is responsible for the narrative of the group. One of my mentors had a mantra which was "The leader is responsible for the narrative". If you are dealing with followers who are under mental health attack, the words you use and the message conveyed can be very important. Let's take a narrative like:

    "We are going through a period of high uncertainty again. This is bad for us and our industry. We will have to try and cope, like we did last time with whatever happens. These are bad conditions. We had better wait and see what happens. I will let you know if I get any news." Or the same situation might be:

    "We are going through a period of exciting change. While this presents challenges to our industry, we are at the forefront and we are good at dealing with change. I expect we will adapt and move faster than most, and secure the most gains as we did last time we were in this situation. These are bad conditions for our competitors but ideal for us. I can't wait for us to get stuck into this. I will update you tomorrow, but in the meantime I have every confidence that we will all rise to the challenge and do a great job."

An example of the recognition of the contemporary importance of the 'narrative' is from Sir Nicholas Carter, former Chief of the General Staff (Head of the British Army):

> "Success is more likely to be achieved through non-military or non-lethal means, and invariably it is the triumph of the narrative that is decisive, not necessarily the facts on the ground".

Further reading: Army Doctrine Publication, Land Operations. Ministry of Defence, UK. 2017.

7. GET CLOSE. We all hide behind our roles, titles, experiences and the façade we construct for ourselves in our working lives. The best leaders are able to break through this and connect on a deeper level with their followers. While doing this, the leader may be able to uncover the 'All Blacks' (Chapter 4) of their followers, and in doing so, build trust as well as see a way forward to help the followers to deal with their 'All Blacks'. Even if no action comes from this, often the follower feels cared for, or understood, and does not feel alone.
8. PROVIDE MORE RESOURCES. Most problems can be moved forward with more resources. This might be more money, or more people, or more kit, or all of these. If more resources are invested, followers feel that the problem is being taken seriously, their load reduces and their confidence in success increases. Of course, they need to be the right resources targeted in the right way, but then that is when the experience of the leader counts.
9. TREATS. My experience is that treats have a disproportionate effect on followers' morale, mental health and performance. The leader turning up with chocolates, beers, cakes or pizza often works well. The fact that the leader has thought about this and organised it themselves often goes a long way. It appeals to our childlike senses and is a bit naughty, and can provide some respite from the challenges in hand. Timing is critical, don't turn up at the wrong time and distract.
10. KINDNESS. Another type of act that seems to have disproportionate impact are acts of kindness, particularly if it is unexpected. Often the wives/husbands/partners of staff experiencing mental health attack at work, carry an unseen

burden. One thing I have seen is a leader sending flowers/wine to the wives/husbands/partners of managers who are under strain – with a note "we know it's a tough time – thank you for your support". No big announcements are needed but the impact on wellbeing can be huge. Sometimes just turning up after something big and bad has happened, and just saying "is everyone OK?", is powerful.

11. LIGHTEN THE LOAD. If the load can be lightened, followers will feel an immediate release of burden and often a surge of energy. Lightening the load could be things like:

    - Reducing the workload
    - Moving the deadlines
    - Clarifying priorities
    - Changing priorities
    - Changing expectations about performance.

    You can also encourage your followers to do this for their followers.

12. TELL THE TRUTH. In a work situation under stress, people will build up multiple narratives about what has happened, what is happening and what is going to happen. Often armed with half-truths, and fuelled by mis-communications and gossip, things can often get far from the actual position. If the leader sets out the picture as they see it in an honest way, not only are the followers armed with reality, but you move from multiple narratives to one. In my experience most followers can deal with a certain truth, no matter how bad, if delivered with hope, rather than multiple half-truths fuelling uncertainty and doubt.

13. SHOW COURAGE. When the chips are down, followers are very receptive to having their mental health boosted by displays of courage from the leader. Military examples of this are obvious, but in a business it might mean meeting face to face with the staff and delivering some bad news in person, rather than sending a messenger. It might be sharing the burden of long hours. It might be taking on those even higher up, at personal risk, to protect and safeguard your followers. As well as physical courage, we can talk about moral courage, the courage to make the right decision, even though it might bring risk and pain

to the leader, but will be to the benefit of the whole. Taking responsibility for a subordinate's mistakes in a board meeting, to cover for them, but in doing so exposing you, is an example of moral courage, or simply expressing your view when all others have agreed to go the opposite way. I was on a board once seeking Angel/VC capital, and having previously hit the sales targets, late in the deal process, after the price had been agreed but before the process was signed off; the business missed a sales target. The board decided to offer the investors a better deal (worse for the board and existing shareholders, better for the new investors). This took courage from the board to have to sell this to all shareholders but it was the right thing to do, and it built trust. It is fundamental to leadership; people will follow others who base their decision making on what is right as opposed to what is convenient or personally rewarding.

14. TAKE OUT THE 'TERRORISTS'. Whatever organisation you are in, a school, factory, an office, a dance company, when the going gets tough and stress levels rise, there will be some people who actually escalate the stress for others. They are often a very small percentage of the workforce, but account for a disproportionate impact. They will go around sometimes as merchants of doom and gloom, sometimes as wingers or gossipers, and spread stress like a virus. Sometimes they will do this consciously, often they will not be aware they are doing it. These people need to be taken out of the front line. Remove them, move them to the back of the line, redeploy, tie them up with other tasks, or make them redundant, just get them out of where the action is hottest. Often they can be people who are unconscious and will not support any stress boosting measures. In fact they might well go around when you the leader are not there, and deliberately mis-interpret what you have said. I know it's emotive and non-PC but I call these people 'terrorists'. Deal with them. But be careful. I have also learnt that sometimes your biggest critic in the moment, can be your biggest supporter in the long run, if led well. I have personally experienced this. Don't blame the complainer if they are suffering from lack of leadership! A terrorist could be a freedom fighter who could be on your side!

15. THANK YOU. Apart from OK, thank you is the most powerful leadership phrase. It is especially powerful if you go out of your way to say it in person and is unexpected. Of course it must be genuine. It probably will be unexpected as despite it being so simple, it is also so rare. For the cleaner to be thanked by the head teacher, for the charity volunteer by the charity CEO, for the private to be thanked by the general, these things go a long way. What is more, the subordinate will tell everyone it has happened.

So here are 15 strategies you can use as **stress busters and mental health boosters** with your followers. Remember their mental health is your responsibility. Which of the fifteen can you immediately deploy?

	Stress buster / mental health booster	Tip:	
1	Example	Light the fire of example: deploy the 100 Action Station! points on you.	
2	Encourage	Encourage your followers to deploy the 100 Action Stations! points on them.	
3	Turn up (and say something)	Be visible, be interested, and be prepared to get close to the action.	
4	Have a plan	Make sure your followers know you have a plan and make sure they know what they have to do. Change the plan as you go.	
5	Momentum	Follow up good news and positives with other positives to build forward momentum.	
6	Narrative	The leader carries the narrative – make sure it is a realistic, positive and an optimistic one.	
7	Get close	Understand your followers 'All Blacks' and then act on this intelligence.	
8	Provide more resources	More resources directed to the areas of critical need can mean that the job gets done faster, better or cheaper.	
9	Treats	Bring smiles to the followers' faces.	
10	Kindness	Unexpected acts of kindness, deliver disproportionate results.	

	Stress buster / mental health booster	Tip:	
11	Lighten the load	Take work away, extend the time line, change priorities and expectations.	
12	Tell the truth	Replace the multiple narratives with one.	
13	Show courage	Share the risk and show physical and moral courage.	
14	Take out the 'terrorists'	Correctly identify and then remove from the context people who are escalating stress for others.	
15	Thank you	Go out of your way to say it, and mean it.	

CHAPTER 10: CHALLENGES FOR FUTURE LEADERS

This chapter is written for Future Leaders.

Conventionally Future Leaders have been interpreted as young people with the potential and desire to lead. At Nelsonspirit, we define a Future Leader as any young person 17-24 years who aspires to lead in business, charity, public service or in their community. In the Nelsonspirit community we believe that is it the duty of the leaders of today to encourage the leaders of tomorrow. However, this assumes a model where the context is static and a younger generation takes over the reins from the older. If the future is changing fast, and as some would suggest exponentially, then we will all need to be "Future Leaders" in spirit, if we are to achieve the objective of dealing with stress, improving mental health and improving performance.

The interesting thing about leadership is that some of it is timeless. It relates to every generation. This is why the examples of heroes from history can be powerful. While every generation believes it is unique and different, the fundamentals of human behaviour remain the same over the centuries. Inspiration, courage, humility, trust, vision, respect are all examples, which glow equally bright in leaders of all generations. However, contexts do change and therefore the tools that are needed for the leader change too. Maybe in the future, we will need to deploy some old tools in new ways or discover completely new ways of dealing with things. So what does the future landscape look like for future leaders? Where are the likely potential attacks on mental health coming from? How best should we deal with potential attacks on our mental health and that of our followers?

Working with future leaders I have identified four challenges that potentially will create stress and disrupt mental health in the future. These are four mental health challenges for Future Leaders. It should help everyone who aspires to lead in the future, to understand what the future might look like. With information technology, the future is arriving faster than it has in the past! These challenges threaten to either attack the health of the future leader, or the health of the future leader's followers. Undealt with, they will harm us, by delivering XStress and overloading, leading to a deterioration in both mental health and performance. So how should we prepare for them? If we can anticipate the threat we can have the response ready, and in some cases may be able to turn the situation into one that boosts mental health and performance.

The four mental health challenges for the future, dealing with:

The mental health attack from the changing nature of work.
The mental health attack from the changing nature of information.
The mental health attack from the emergence of identity.
The mental health attack from tomorrow's technology.

CHALLENGE 1 - THE MENTAL HEALTH ATTACK FROM THE CHANGING NATURE OF WORK

The context

In the 1950s, after National Service, my dad joined the Norwich Union Insurance Company in Norwich (now known as Aviva). He spent his entire career with them, rising from tea boy to a senior manager. One industry, one company, one location. They provided him with meaningful work, status, identity, pay, pension, a career, training, sickness benefits, social benefits, sporting benefits, medical benefits, annual pay increases, promotion, qualifications, travel, employment protection, meritocratic rise, social mobility and a job for life. In addition, the big hidden benefit was that his health and wellbeing were well supported by the organisation and Norwich Union proved to be a great company to work for. His grandchildren will not walk over a similar bridge. There are not as many of these "one-industry, one-company, one-location" bridges left. Information, Communications and Entertainment Technology (ICE Tech) revolution has blown these bridges!

If I compare the world of work for my father, with the world of work for my children, there are some interesting changes we can observe. My dad might be shocked or surprised to discover today:

More part time work.
More older people are working.
More women in the workforce.

More diversity in the workplace.
24/7 working.
Working from home.
Working from abroad.
Move away from one job to multiple jobs.
Move away from one-wage households.
More people caring for family outside work.
Zero hours contracts.
More people taking gap periods / time away.
Expectations and behaviour of generations X, Y, Z Millennials (whoever they are!).
Real wages stagnant for many, big pay rises for a few.
Growth of the sharing economy.
Growth of the gig economy.
Growth of the black/hidden economy.
Employment/work growth outside organisations.
Business sizes polarizing into the very big and the very small.
Big used to be regional/national, it's now international/global.
Structural changes in the work that is available.
Psychological contract changing in relation to pensions and benefits.
Work moving from somewhere we go to, to something we do.

An interesting insight is provided by Charles Handy who in his 1995 book 'The Empty Raincoat' predicted many of these changes, something he reviewed in his most recent book 'The Second Curve'. Handy is one of my academic heroes and a man who has been at the forefront of thinking about the changing nature of work for decades.

Further reading: The Empty Raincoat: Making Sense of the Future. 1995. Charles Handy. The Second Curve: Thoughts on Reinventing Society. 2016. Charles Handy

The threat

Many of these outcomes are driven by the ICE Tech (Information, Communications and Entertainment Technology) revolution. Many of the changes listed above threaten to undermine mental health. For example, having staff working on their own from home or remotely most of the time is not good for their health. Many of these factors point to the demise of the "organisation" as the one-stop-shop for all our social engagement needs. Part of this historical package was that the organisation protected us and secured our mental health, and provided us with social situations so we could maintain our mental health. Work was much like being on a luxury ocean liner, we were well protected from the elements and the dangers of the sea. You could work up the ranks and end up at the captain's table. Above all, the luxury liner provided comfort, social interaction and security. Many of us now work from canoes, rafts, temporary boats or pleasure craft, highly exposed to the vagaries of the winds and the sea.

The future leader's responsibilities will be to recognise the loss of support and protection previously afforded by the large social organisation, and organise the supply of these things from elsewhere, i.e. leaders will need to replace the social and personal support that organisations used to provide in other ways. We are already seeing record numbers of networking groups/hackathons/business groups/flash groups than ever before, and these provide opportunities for interaction and support for those who work on their own or in small units. We are also seeing record numbers of communities form, many online. We also have vloggers, bloggers and tweeters amassing huge followings. The future leader's role will be to make sure their people are plugged into these groups and where appropriate to link up their enterprise with others into a convoy. We are moving from a 'battleship and cruiser fleet' to a 'convoy of little ships', maybe guarded by, and serving, the mega-mother-ship. We will still need a fleet; we will still need leadership; work will still need to be done, but the new ships will look very different to old ones. People will organise themselves and communicate in very different ways. The large organisation used to be the main provider of work and leadership opportunities but this might is not be the case in the future. As work is leaving the luxury liner, so leadership might leave too. Future Leaders might well be people who do not have senior roles in big organisations, but lead new communities forming in the new industries, enabling social interaction and providing security in new ways.

The attack from the changing nature of work, and the leadership challenge for future leaders:

> The future leader will need to provide social interaction and security for their followers in new ways, previously provided by the place where our fore fathers worked: the social organisation.

CHALLENGE 2 - THE MENTAL HEALTH ATTACK FROM THE CHANGING NATURE OF INFORMATION

The context

We are having to deal with more and more information at work, and this is coming at us at faster and faster rates. Information, in many ways, has become the new dominating 'factor of production'. Moore's law from electronic processors say processing speeds double every 2 years. Many experts believe that this is happening to information. Not only is this attack at work, it is also happening in our personal lives, and many people are plugged into their phone, especially the young, for their social life too! Most managers have 200+ emails a day, many of these are via the dreaded cc! (Which incidentally stands for carbon copy, from when a piece of carbon paper was put behind the top sheet so as you penned the top copy, an inked version would appear on the bottom copy!) Most managers check their phone 100s of times a day. Most people do this outside work hours. Some do not even have "work hours". Gone are the days when my dad returned home at 17.45 for dinner cooked by mum, for an evening with the family or doing hobbies, and only very occasionally he would bring a brief case of work home. In the work with leaders I have found in the last 2 years most leaders and their followers have reached the tipping point of information overload. There is too much of it, and many people are struggling to clear it. Information is coming in faster than we can deal with it. This speed of information flow has caught many off guard and the skills of sifting and filtering have often not kept pace with the incoming. Not only has the quantity and speed of information increasing exponentially, the quality of it has also started to vary considerably. In recent times there has been an increase in "fake news / mis information" (and what we used to call propaganda!). The systems that we have within our organisations are not coping with this new quantity, speed and quality of information. The risk of information loss, corruption and theft has now increased so there is now a higher priority on information security. Social media platforms have allowed business policy, and reputations to be projected and attacked, at high speed.

What you know and what you don't know about people, organisations and situations is becoming an interesting area. A quote from the ex head of MI5/6 that I like is: "Intelligence is something that someone does not want you to know!" States and organisations have always had the capability and power to project information, this power has now been democratised so individuals are able to use, misuse and abuse this power too.

For inspiration we can look back at the great work done at Bletchley Park during WW2, with Alan Turing and others, cracking the Enigma code. This 'impossible to solve code' had 159 million million million combinations, but Turing and his team cracked it and it is claimed they shortened the war by two years. Churchill said Turing had more influence on the war than any other single individual. Turing and an eclectic gang of many others did this by applying new and creative ways of thinking about the problem.

"Hero of the past: Alan Turing – cracking the enigma code"

The threat

The role of information and how it plays on our minds psychologically is an emerging and real threat. You might like to revisit the earlier commentary on the role of the subconscious and the activity of the chimp.

Having too much information – can damage mental health *(Quantity).*
Having information coming in faster than you can deal with it – can damage mental health *(Speed).*
Not having the right/truthful information – can damage mental health *(Quality).*
The management information systems, MIS, at work that we have to help us deal with information are broken *(Inadequate MIS)* – which can damage mental health.

There is constant and looming threat of costly breaches of information *(Security)* - which can damage mental health.

The leader is in a unique place to bring the issue of information and its impact on health and performance to the top of the agenda. As the carrier of the narrative and the beacon of personal example, they can shape the way others deal with information. Above all, the future leader can sponsor and authorise the design and implementation of new information systems. This might be by using IT architecture or it could be as simple as telling staff not to cc reports, or limit board notes to one page not 40! All this can release time and space for both health to improve and performance to rise. Earlier we spoke about everyone having an opinion but the best opinion being independent, expert and informed. Future leaders will have to work at being independent, expert and informed and then carrying the narrative of the truth.

The attack from the changing nature of information, and the leadership challenge for future leaders:

> The future leader will need to will need to understand the link between information, health and performance, and set an example in personal information management. They will need to carry the narrative of truth and lead the design of new management information systems that can deal with the quantity, quality, speed and security of information.

CHALLENGE 3 - THE MENTAL HEALTH ATTACK FROM THE EMERGENCE OF IDENTITY

The context

I grew up back in the 1970s, in Norwich. Like most in the City at that time, I was born in the City and it had been that way for many generations. I grew up in the shadow of WW2 and outside sport I can't remember identity really being an issue for the first half of my life. I grew up proud to be from Norwich and Norfolk and of course I was also English and British. Being patriotic was acceptable and great fun. Identity only really mattered when it came to sport. If it was Football – Come on England; Rugby – Come on England; Cricket – Come on England. Scotland of course were the arch enemy, hated, and never to be supported ... unless of course they formed the British Curling team at the

Winter Olympics, and then we loved the Scots, ate short bread and got out the tartan. Every true Englishman, Scotsman, Irishman or Welshman knows the paradox of the national identity question, and it is perfectly normal to knock the stuffing out of each other one week, and then form up as the British Lions the next week! English and British were used interchangeably, nobody really discussed, or was bothered either way, about being Europeans, although we had just joined a customs area called the EEC, which we were told would be good for trade with those exotic folk across the channel the 'Continentals'. We had the confidence of knowing that matters of identity were given. 'We' was greater than 'I', this is what got us through the war, and anyway, no true Englishman would be so rude as to go around asserting his difference. I might be looking back on my childhood with rose-tinted spectacles, and we now know that not everything in the 1970s behind the scenes was good, but interestingly looking back, I would say that my mental health and that of my friends was very high.

We hear a lot today about generation of X,Y,Z and Millennials, and the advertising industry gets very excited although very few people seem to want to publically self-identify with these groups. At times I feel a bit left out so I am now claiming a category for me and my age group, The Blue Peter Generation. As a child, one of my heroes was TV presenter John Noakes. John was an enthusiastic and proud Yorkshireman, an adult with a childlike love of the world, and particularly for having a go at new things. The other presenters Peter Purves and Valerie Singleton, were more like your parents: loving, wise and above all, sensible. John was the free spirit and in a much simpler age would go off and do all sorts of crazy things, like being the first civilian to parachute freefall 5 miles; bob sleigh the Cresta Run; or build a James Bond set from cereal packets, squeezy liquid bottles, sticky tape and sticky-back-plastic. Experts (such as Percy Edwards or Precious McKenzie) and authority figures, were respected and reverentially listened to and it did not matter who you were, anyone could get a Blue Peter badge, if you did some good. Leaders are people who inspire others to get stuff done, and John inspired me. One episode he climbed a ladder in Trafalgar Square to the top of Nelson's column to clean it, without safety line or insurance. He did this in his normal cheery, can-do way, making slight of the difficulties and risks. It would certainly not be allowed today. It seemed a much simpler world then.

Today things seem a bit more complicated. Today who and what you are, have become very important for some people. I wonder what John would have made of the recent accusations that Nelson was a racist slave-supporting supremacist and that Nelson's Column should be torn down! In the last 30 years the concept of diversity has been has entered the workplace, and in many ways, this has been a good thing. Communities built on diversity, and mutual respect of difference, are usually stronger than those built on similarity, ignorance and prejudice. But along with diversity, has come 'political correctness' and an obsession that many have with identity.

Identity is about who and what YOU are, and how important it is for others to know this, respect it, and accommodate it. The national media seems obsessed with accommodation of the minorities by the majority, or at least a provocation of the majority, by presenting outrages from the minority. Everyone now seems to be part of a minority, and part of some separatist agenda. Alongside this, the concepts of personal and celebrity brand have grown in visibility. Even the word 'community' has been hijacked. In the 1970s community was the people who lived in your area, and if anyone needed help, the community provided it. Community was about all of us, and caring for each other. I knew I could rely on the people in our community and they could rely on me. Today we hear talk about the Business community, the Muslim community, the Gay community, the Green community, the Investment community, the Asian community etc – the subtext being 'people not like you who are likely to cause trouble or be opposed to you'. Which is sad. Communities of interest can be built faster than ever before, particularly on line, and this can be good, but in some ways community has moved from something which was a positive socio-geographical feature to a troublesome sub group that other people, not like you, identify with.

At the same time, identity politics has become a big issue in the media. Whether it be sexuality (LGBT), or gender (male, female, trans, zee), or race or religion, and idiotically the whole county has split into whether you are a Brexiteer or Remoaner! I am not saying that these things are not important for the individual, and I recognise for some they are very important, but it is fuelling an attack on mental health, we now have a workface where for some people identity is a big issue, and this presents a new challenge for the leader.

The threat

Central to leadership is the idea of bringing people together to rally behind a cause greater than self. If people are treating 'self' with much more importance, this makes it harder for mainstream leaders to form groups of followers or manage their followers. In addition, followers might be attracted to more extreme leaders who champion the more extreme views that separatist and minority groups attract. Selective media filtering will make it much easier for those with a grievance or hatred towards others to find and follow an extremist leader. Not all future leaders would get a Blue Peter badge. Despite this, many (good) leaders, particularly in public life and in large organisations have a very small or weak following and are only being propped up in their role by positional power or media support. We live in a world of fading deference and fading immediate acquiescence to authority. Things are questioned and open to much more comment and analysis. While some of this is probably good, it is also a world where any crackpot can galvanise a following online and create momentum for a cause, stir up hatred, bring discomfort or threat. My view is that identity is driving mental health problems as we set people up against each other, because we are different, and we have a national narrative that is accelerating poor mental health in this way.

Leaders bring people together regardless of difference. Some leadership will be within communities of difference, but the real challenge and opportunity will be across difference. These are the new bridges that need to be built to bring together communities that are not same. At a very simple level, your followers might be a much more mixed bag than they have been in the past, so being sensitive to culture, history, gender, background, sexuality etc. might become a more important skill for the future leader. The leader will have a key role in identifying and bringing people together to form communities.

The attack from the emergence of identity, and the leadership challenge for future leaders:

The future leader will need to solve the riddle, wrapped in a mystery, inside an enigma (Churchill) that is identity. This will involve a recognition that followers might well be of a diverse and eclectic mix, and some of those will need their difference recognised; but at the same time a community of 'WE' to address a higher purpose will need to be built. Future leaders will need to be both more sensitive to difference, yet stronger and faster at building a community focused on a higher purpose.

CHALLENGE 4 - THE MENTAL HEALTH ATTACK FROM TOMORROW'S TECHNOLOGY

The context

Any analysis of the future is problematic, especially when it comes to technology. We have always had technology, like we have always had leadership. Both shape our working world and both simultaneously cause and help us deal with the problems that we face. Most future predictions have a common feature of being almost completely wrong. At school, I was told that when we got to work, there would be a computer on every desk (true, but it took longer) and this would take over a lot of the work that humans had previously done (true) and so we would only need to work 3 days a week, and most of our lives would be full of leisure (ha ha!).

But if we accept that we are going through the ICE Tech revolution (some call it the Fourth Industrial Revolution), and if we accept that things are speeding up, then the impact on mental health and performance and the leader's role in shaping both, becomes key. A leading thinker in the fourth industrial revolution is Klaus Schwab:

"The changes are so profound that, from the perspective of human history, there has never been a time of greater promise or potential peril. The fourth industrial revolution is characterized by a range of new technologies that are fusing the physical, digital and biological worlds, impacting all disciplines, economies and industries, and even challenging ideas about what it means to be human. The world has the potential to connect billions more people to digital networks, dramatically improve the efficiency of organizations and even manage assets in ways that can help regenerate the natural environment, potentially undoing the damage of previous industrial revolutions."

However, Schwab also has grave concerns: that organizations might be unable to adapt; governments could fail to employ and regulate new technologies to capture their benefits; shifting power will create important new security concerns; inequality may grow; and societies fragment. At the heart of his analysis is the conviction that the Fourth Industrial Revolution is within the control of all of us as long as we are able to collaborate across geographies, sectors and disciplines to grasp the opportunities it presents.

Further reading: The Fourth Industrial Revolution. Klaus Schwab. 2017.

The threat

The interesting thing about many of the tech changes just over the horizon, is that they will speed up the intensity of some of the mental health challenges we currently face. If we revisit our equation:

$$\beta\ (P \times \mathbf{D}) > (B \times C)\ 1/\beta$$

We feel stressed when P x D is greater than B x C i.e. when your perceived demands of the situation are greater than your believed capability to safely deal with the situation. This is multiplied up or down, depending on whether you perceive the stress to be helpful or harmful (β). Technology might make D, VERY BIG INDEED, VERY QUICKLY. In fact D might have to re-labelled 'disruption' as the technology might well turn upside down many of the givens in our lives.

With a danger of being laughed at when future generations read this manual in years to come, here are some of the things that experts say will disrupt work and in doing so could provoke a mental health attack:

The internet of things
Cyber security / war
Identity fraud
Robotics
Artificial intelligence
Role of technology in multinationals and the impact on nation states
Virtual reality
Gaming and e-sports
Artificial intelligence
Non national and virtual currencies

Non domicile workers
Nanotechnology
Block chain technology
Genomes technology
Non hard currency payments systems
Quantum computing
Bio technology
Raising capital by crowd funding
Social impact investing, and social finance
Neurology, the mind and technology
Global, local and virtual governance
Autonomous vehicles

Not only are each of these disruptive, there will be interesting white water where the confluence of the rivers of each of these meet. It will be a place of great turbulence, yet great opportunity.

The future leaders' opportunity is to show their followers that they are aware of what is happening, that they have a plan, and that in the new worlds, both health and performance can not only be maintained but improved.

The attack from tomorrow's technology and the leadership challenge for future leaders:

> The future leader will need to show how the adoption of new technology will help people's health and performance. They will have to learn from people and contexts that are not familiar to them. They will also have to reach out to people not in their traditional community of followers. Future threats to health are likely to be multiple, fast and ever changing - and our set of responses will need to be too. And they will need to constantly innovate, be agile and flexible, constantly adjusting their mix of Action Stations to meet the ever-changing new dawn.

SUMMARY

While the future is always hard to predict, it does seem that at present the future is coming at us faster than it did in the past! It will present new challenges of mental health for future leaders. And future leaders will include not only young people, but those of us who aspire to continue to deliver high performance in the future. We will need to brace ourselves for attacks coming from 4 areas:

The mental health attack from the changing nature of work. The future leader will need to provide social interaction and security for their followers in new ways, previously provided by the place where our fore fathers worked: the social organisation.

The mental health attack from the changing nature of information. The future leader will need to understand the link between information, health and performance, and set an example in personal information management. They will need to carry the narrative of truth and lead the design of new management information systems that can deal with the quantity, quality, speed and security of information.

The mental health attack from the emergence of identity. The future leader will need to solve the riddle, wrapped in a mystery, inside an enigma (Churchill) that is identity. This will involve a recognition that followers might well be of a diverse and eclectic mix, and some of those will need their difference recognised, but at the same time a community of 'WE' to address a higher purpose will need to be built. Future leaders will need to be both more sensitive to difference, yet stronger and faster at building a community focused on a higher purpose.

The mental health attack from tomorrow's technology. The future leader will need to show how the adoption of new technology will help people's health and performance. They will have to learn from people and contexts that are not familiar to them. They will also have to reach out to people not in their traditional community of followers. Future threats to health are likely to be multiple, fast and ever changing - and our set of responses will need to be too. And they will need to constantly innovate, be agile and flexible, constantly adjusting their mix of Action Stations to meet the ever changing new dawn.

Remember, the future is coming at us faster than it has in the past. Performance and Leadership will be as important as ever in meeting the challenges of the future. Dealing with stress lies at the heart of both performance and leadership - so let's get everyone to ACTION STATIONS!

100 ACTION STATIONS CHECKLIST

RECOGNITION – ***accepting that you are under a mental health attack and viewing it in different and new ways, to help you deal with it.***			
1	Listen to yourself - "Google your soundtrack". Lay down a positive soundtrack today.		
2	Identify your support network, and bring them to alert.		
3	Form a round table, based around character and capability.	King Arthur	
4	Catch it, Kill it, Cook it, Eat it. Adopt the mindset of a survivalist.	Bear Grylls	
5	You have more, or less time, than you think, both are good.		
6	Accept that you might need to take unprecedented action.	Queen Boudicca	
7	Games can be, and often are, won in "Fergie time".	Alex Ferguson	
8	Go on a Mental Health First Aid course, or speak with someone who has, or read up on it, or simply adopt a First Aid mindset to your mental health.		
9	Engage Enemy More closely - if we are to get better and seize victory, we need to take personal responsibility and get close to the problems.	Admiral Nelson	
10	Refer yourself to the doctor. Then ask for a referral. Do it now, but see it as part of the overall picture not THE answer.		
11	Two heads are better than one - find a health partner.	Rolls Royce	
12	Give yourself good intent. Something like "I intend to get better". Each day, work towards getting better.	GB Ladies Hockey	
13	Reframe 'losing and pain', as 'winning and fun'. Start with trying to have a bit more fun, redefine winning, and then start to believe you can win.		
14	Think freely - deal with the evidence of what is today, not what might be tomorrow.	Thomas Paine	

15	Live in the present, not the past or the future. Focus on enjoying and performing in what you are doing today - leave yesterday and tomorrow alone.		
16	Actively use the most powerful 2 letter word - OK - to deal with acceptance, reflection and action.		
17	Reducing difference reduces stress, but so does being comfortable with difference.		
18	Accept that rationality and irrationality are both imposters. When it comes to your health use both to move you forward.		
19	From fixed to growth mindset - challenge yourself every day - am I limiting myself by adopting fixed mindset? Would it be better to adopt a growth mindset on this?		
20	Recognise that to have a "chimp" as your inner voice is normal, accept that he/she is not the same as you, and keep them in their box.		
21	Syndromitus - use a label to bring focus, but don't let a Mental Health Condition define you.		
22	Be realistic, up to a point.		
23	Be delusional, up to a point.		
24	Recognise that you have "one pie's worth of energy per day" - cut it and eat it wisely.		
25	Minimise the "give away" and "take away" of your time and energy.		
26	Accept that even though you may be weak and feeble in body - you can be strong in spirit.	Elizabeth I	
27	Go to the source of the river - find out where it began and this will help you understand where you are and what you need to do.	Jack Reynolds	
RECOVER – working on actions that give you time and space to think and rest so that you are able to stop things getting worse and put you in a position to move forward.			
28	Build a defence system - information is processed, and responses set in action, to the point of maximum impact.	Lord Dowding	
29	Step up diary management - plan time to recover.		
30	Use the 80/20 rule to deploy resources to stress.		

31	Purpose (I aim to get better) is not enough. To get better it helps to identify what drives you on - why should you get better?	Edith Cavell	
32	Understand how much sleep you need, the impact it has on your operating capability, and work on routines to make sure you get enough.		
33	Use catnaps top "power up": 10-20 minutes will boost you.		
34	Expect the pre-dawn raid, deal with it, roll over.		
35	Identify your "stay awake issue" - and share it.		
36	Turn the kit off - between certain hours - let your phone sleep.		
37	Go for a 'walk and talk' and don't talk about 'it'.		
38	Take the 'monkey' off your back, and don't accept monkeys.		
39	Don't give away power to difficult people - take the initiative, decide in advance how you will engage with them.		
40	Don't try to enlighten the 'unconscious' - their cups are full.		
41	An engaged change is better than a rest. Step up your (displacement) activity.		
42	'Art of Action' - be clear about your intent and link this to a clear response plan; expect things not to go to plan, make decisions close to the action given the unfolding situation.		
43	Accept that you should not empower others with an expectation that they have an answer - you might be disappointed.		
44	Have a 'cobra' meeting - with others or a daily/ weekly solo to review current position, review progress and raise morale.		
45	Control or influence - accept that you can control little, but influence a lot. Be a wise King Canute.	King Canute	
46	Cut the 'salami' - view the whole as a series of digestible chunks.		
47	Play 'one-touch' - deal with a piece of communications only once.		

48	Deploy 'relaxation techniques'. Try them and adopt the ones you enjoy.		
49	If you are a thinker - understand and live life consistent with the 'mental laws'.		
50	De-personalise your situation.		
51	Blend the best of the amateur and professional, and play your health game your way - be true to yourself.	Fred Perry	
52	Step up sport / exercise regime.		
53	Obsess about being a mental athlete, not a mental patient.		
54	Borrow models / paradigms from things that interest you, and construct your health problem within the framework of a world that interests you.		
55	Use routines to help turn yourself 'on and off'.		
56	Hobbies - On the Ball City - step up, take up, or revisit and enjoyable hobby that gets you on the move and enables you to immerse yourself for a short while in another world.		
57	Does it need doing today? If so 'Action this Day' (Churchill) and 'Complete this Day' (Wellington). Otherwise leave until tomorrow.		
58	If you are spending too much time at the fence - don't. Turn off your communications. When there, classify them as they come in. Decide which you will deal with now, and which later.		
59	Make time (10 mins) to be intimate with your partner and care for them each day.		
60	Use Project Management Methodology - use time, cost/resource, scope and risk to plan for a great recovery.		
61	From Slim - get yourself a good recovery plan, be flexible about it, and limit discussion about it.	General Bill Slim	
RESPOND - responses that will directly help you get better.			
62	Help others - it helps yourself.	Dr Hal Belknap	
63	Recognise the thinking-feeling-doing link. Start feeling better by thinking better.		

64	Deeds not words - it's the actions you take that change things.	Emily Wilding Davison	
65	Do something to boost your mental health, then go online and talk about it for amplification.		
66	Go neutral - decide not to respond, or just say no.		
67	Surround yourself with disciplined people and be disciplined in your thoughts and disciplined in your actions.		
68	Spit out the 'marbles' because you need to.		
69	Use 'blocking out' in your diary. To rest, recover, think or manoeuvre.		
70	Like BP, use improvisation and creativity to impact both how you feel and how others see you - both helps our health	Baden Powell	
71	Compartmentalise and time box your work, to allow focus and breaks from your main issue.		
72	Formally and informally share thoughts with your 'band of brothers'.		
73	Ask not how much did I fail, but how much did I learn? Analyse all activity in terms of learning not failure. Learn something new.		
74	Practice 'mindfulness' either as a formal technique or at least be aware of your thoughts and fill your mind FULL of positive thoughts.		
75	Go back to basics - 'bounce hit'. Simplify and strip back to the essential components of good health. Concentrate on getting them right.		
76	Be like Gandhi - disobey your illness.	Mahatma Gandhi	
77	Stay off the drugs unless prescribed by a doctor, and even then view drugs as part of the short term solution not the whole long term solution.		
78	Go for a 'walk and talk' and talk about 'it'.		
79	Speak to your mentor - engage with them more closely.		
80	Step up your nutrition. You are what you eat. Eat more nutritious food.		

81	Count your blessings by making a list that you re-work.		
82	Do what you enjoy - list, diary, action.		
83	Don't own it - you cannot solve a problem that is not yours. Drop the banana.		
84	Actively use the 'garden of the subconscious'.		
85	Do normal things and track your progress to 'more' normal.		
86	Be open and transparent with others - they will surprise you with how much they can help.		
87	Ask for help - and tell people how they can help.		
88	Accept that you are not alone, you are normal. Reach out and share.		
89	Smile more - it's good for you and for others. It beats the alternative.		
90	'Get a laugh on'. Laugh more. Surround yourself with people who make you laugh. Make others laugh.	Ken Dodd	
91	Move more, and if you can, move more outdoors.		
92	Delegate, abdicate or dump - be sensitive to whether these reduce stress or actually increase stress and for whom.		
93	Go to the dump. Write stuff down. Keep a notebook.		
94	Use urgent and important list or do difficult first.		
95	'Graffiti' - express yourself in colour on the wall.		
96	If you are in a tight spot, identify some 'vital mental medicine' - music or entertainment that will raise your spirits.	Ernest Shackleton	
97	Give someone a warm hug or stand them a drink.	Mr Tilley	
98	Get the sand in your toes, the wind on your face, and a fire glow into your eyes.		
99	Keep going, sometimes being free from illness takes a long time.	William Wilberforce	
100	Put things in perspective and do your best to survive the day as best you can.	Alistair Urquhart	

READERS NOTES

PHOTOGRAPHIC ACKNOWLEDGEMENTS

Page 10: © Nigel Cushion
Page 17: © Andy Fisher
Page 21: www.iwm.org.uk/collections/item/object/205015977 from the collections of the Imperial War Museums. Crown copyright expired
Page 42: © Mikołaj Bleja. Licensed by Pexels (www.pexels.com)
Page 57: © Waseem Farooq. Licensed under Creative Commons, via Pxhere (pxhere.com)
Page 59: www.iwm.org.uk/collections/item/object/205195019) from the collections of the Imperial War Museums. Crown copyright expired
Page 66: public domain, via Wikimedia Commons
Page 67: © Kalei Brooks. Public domain, via Wikimedia Commons
Page 69: licensed under Creative Commons, via Wikimedia Commons
Page 70: © Gordon Flood. Licensed under Creative Commons, via Wikimedia Commons
Page 72: © Redcoat. Licensed under Creative Commons, via Wikimedia Commons
Page 74: both photos © Arnaud 25. Licensed under Creative Commons, via Wikimedia Commons
Page 77: public domain, via Wikimedia Commons
Page 84: © CloW. Licensed under Creative Commons, via Wikimedia Commons
Page 86: public domain, via Wikimedia Commons
Page 89: © J.D. Noske / Anefo. Licensed under Creative Commons, via Wikimedia Commons
Page 93: © nikoretro. Licensed under Creative Commons, via Wikimedia Commons
Page 96: public domain, via Wikimedia Commons
Page 103: © Sanath Adiga. Public domain, via Good Free Photos (www.goodfreephotos.com)
Page 110: public domain, via Wikimedia Commons
Page 116: © Nigel Cushion
Page 117: © Nigel Cushion
Page 125: public domain, via Wikimedia Commons. Crown copyright expired
Page 129: © JoAnn Belknap
Page 131: public domain, via Wikimedia Commons
Page 133: © Nigel Cushion
Page 137: public domain, via Wikimedia Commons
Page 141: public domain, via Wikimedia Commons
Page 143: © Nigel Cushion
Page 151: © University of Liverpool Faculty of Health & Life Sciences. Licensed under Creative Commons, via Wikimedia Commons
Page 154: © Frank Hurley. Public domain, via Wikimedia Commons
Page 155: © Frank Hurley. Public domain, via Wikimedia Commons
Page 156: © Alex Tilley
Page 158: public domain, via Wikimedia Commons
Page 165: © Mikołaj Bleja. Licensed by Pexels (www.pexels.com)
Page 181: © Loz Pycock. Licensed under Creative Commons, via creativecommons.org
Page 199: © Nigel Cushion

POSTSCRIPT

I have found that by deploying these Action Points I was able to improve my own stress management, improve my mental health and improve my performance by 20%, and I believe you can too. Others have tried these actions and they work. What might happen if we brought the whole nation to Action Stations? According to the experts, poor mental health is costing the nation £105bn per annum. The tax take on an increase of 20% productivity is £122bn. The current NHS budget is £127bn. Conclusion: the effect of getting the Nation to Action Stations is an amount equivalent to nearly double the NHS budget! What a fork in the road that would be.

If you would like to join me on the fork in the road, have found any of this manual useful, can think of how I could improve the manual, or you have just enjoyed reading it, do let me know. Comments for improvement are great for my learning, and positive compliments boost self esteem, so either way it's good for my mental health!

nigel@nigelcushion.co.uk

With the 100 actions in mind, I leave you with quotations from three of my favourite heroes:

> As Shackleton returned to Elephant Island, 100 years ago by boat, after his 3 month Antarctic rescue, he counted the bodies standing on the shore to greet him; all had survived... and then he shouted ashore one question "All's well?" The response came back "All's well Boss, all's well". This is the leader's number one job – to make sure **"All's well..."**
>
> As Shakespeare said - **"All's well that ends well".** When dealing with your stress and mental health, keep the end in mind. It might take a long time to get there ... but you can start today ...
>
> And let's end where we started, make a start now, to get to Action Stations, as Churchill said ... **"Action this Day"!**

Nigel Cushion BSc (Hons), FRSA, is a specialist in Leadership and Mentoring.

Nigel has over 35 years experience in leadership. He started his leadership journey as a volunteer in Scouting, and has gone on to chair many fast growth businesses. He is the former runner-up in the national awards for Non-Executive Chairman in the UK. He has mentored many CEOs and MDs and has spoken on leadership all over the world. He is a Leadership Fellow, St George's House, Windsor Castle, is founder of a leadership mentoring business Nelsonspirit, and runs a trust fund to encourage future leaders.

His work in recent years has led him to realise that dealing with stress and mental health is the number one issue facing leaders today. By blending his own experience with insight from how the best leaders of the past and leaders of today have dealt with stress, he was inspired to write this 'how to' manual. www.nigelcushion.co.uk

He lives in Norfolk with his family.

A percentage of any profits of this book will go to the Nelsonspirit Future Leaders Fund, to encourage young people to grow as leader while helping others.